Instructor's Manual

for

Writing from Life: Collecting and Connecting

by

PHYLLIS BALLATA

Copyright © 1997 by Mayfield Publishing Company

All rights reserved. No portion of this book may be reproduced in any form or by any means without written permission of the publisher.

International Standard Book Number: 1-55934-556-X

Manufactured in the United States of America

10 9 8 7 6 5 4 3 2 1

Mayfield Publishing Company
1280 Villa Street
Mountain View, California 94041

CONTENTS

Preface iv

PART ONE Theory, Organization, and Practical Information   1

A Letter to Colleagues   1

Writing from Life: Collecting and Connecting Text Plan   4

Advantages of the Writing Project Method for Teaching Writing   6

How to Use the Thinking Skills Checklist   8

Sample Syllabus   10

Sample Writing Projects   19

Drills   25

Lesson Plan Chart   27

Alternative Syllabi Ideas   30

Classroom Guidelines   34

PART TWO Reference Charts   39

Writing Project Reference Charts   39

Reading Reference Charts   76

Rhetorical Methods Used in Each Writing Project

Reading and Writing Projects Organized by Rhetorical Methods   102

PREFACE

This manual is divided into two parts, the first covering the theory, organization, and practical information you need to teach your course using *Writing from Life: Collecting and Connecting*, and the second offering a multitude of ways to access the particular projects and readings that you need.

In Part One, I take the opportunity to explain the plan of the text and to reiterate the benefits of the Writing Project Method for teaching writing. The checklist of thinking skills that I have provided can be duplicated for your students. I have also included a recent syllabus that I have developed for use with *Writing from Life*. Of course, it reflects my school's calendar and the areas I choose to emphasize. It is offered as a way of stimulating your thinking about the variety of uses you can make of *Writing from Life* in a semester or a quarter. I have also included suggested in-class writing projects and drills. In addition, a sample lesson plan chart shows a way not only to plan for each class but to use the current term's experience to plan for the next term. I have also created alternative syllabi suggestions for those teaching composition courses organized around various themes or issues. The last section of Part One comprises classroom guidelines that I hope will be particularly helpful for graduate students or first-time teachers who might need some advice on such practicalities as organizing journal responses and grading.

For Part Two, I have tried to summarize important information about the writing projects and the readings in such a way that you will be able to quickly access the sections that most fit your needs and have a handy place to record your observations, opinions, and personal variations of assignments. For each writing project I have listed the author of the short comment that forms the basis of the project, the key ideas, the rhetorical methods, the readings that may be connected to the project, and a space for your comments and notes. For each reading, I have listed the author, title, and date, the key ideas, the rhetorical methods, the difficulty level, and a space for your comments and notes. Next are charts listing each writing project and reading and the rhetorical methods each selection illustrates or can be used to practice. Finally, I have listed for each rhetorical method every writing project and reading that involves that method. My hope is that by presenting the information about the contents of the book in so many ways, I will enable you to pick out the projects and readings best suited to your interests and goals. *Writing from Life* and this manual are intended to be flexible and stimulating resources to enhance your work with reading, thinking, and writing.

PART ONE
THEORY, ORGANIZATION, AND PRACTICAL INFORMATION

A Letter to Colleagues

Dear Friends,

How tiresome it is to put on a show for a sea of bland or blank faces, all waiting for enlightenment from the fount of wisdom, or perhaps simply waiting for the end of the class period. And how discouraging it is to watch the blind leading the blind in the writing "process" or to watch the mental withdrawal of those who are too quick or too slow for the discussion at hand.

Yet the stimulation and joy of teaching and learning are so vital to living that we can't allow them to slip away. In my struggle, I have evolved an intensely focused Writing Project Method. In this method students are asked to confront and respond to the actual words of another mind and heart speaking to them, and the response is focused specifically. The commonly used technique of general response journaling can be helpful for attentive and motivated students, but the results are too often haphazard—I didn't know what to say; I couldn't find anything interesting; I didn't read the poem/story/essay but this is what I think anyway; I didn't know what you wanted; I thought I could just write about anything I wanted to. Most of us have been here before.

The focused Writing Project or response is designed to help me, as a teacher and a learner, *solve several specific and common problems in both teaching and learning:*

1. Poor or nonexistent background in history, science, philosophy, culture, or ethics among all students of all levels of intelligence, age, and skill. For students this weakness causes a helpless feeling of floating separated from all other times and places, a free fall from nowhere into nowhere. For the teacher it causes a sense of hopelessness at the amount of information that should be covered in order to understand the readings or literature as well as the impossibility of covering it in the space of a quarter/semester/year.

2. A cultural lack of alertness and mindfulness; the inability to *see;* and a weakness in the "perceptive faculty" in learning, living, and working.

3. The practical difficulties of engaging classrooms of students who include advanced and slow, young and old, experienced and inexperienced, helpless and skillful, motivated and unmotivated, interested and "bored," clueless and knowledgeable.

4. My compulsion as a teacher to care about both the students and the ideas and yet to give each student responsibility for himself or herself.

The Writing Project Method works in the real world. It provides background through key ideas rather than exhaustive readings (which are so many in number and scope that they cannot be done in the time allowed). The key ideas are used to prompt discussions of contributing background information and, just as important, to connect the human condition of other times and places to the humanity of the student in his or her time and place. The quotations are from real minds, real people living in specific times and places and confronting universal human issues and questions. The connections work for all skill levels, ages, and interests. Anyone can (and everyone should) respond to them.

Because most Writing Projects are done in class (in the teaching design that I use), everyone *must* actively respond to the idea on the spot, perhaps use that response for immediate discussion, and put the writing into their file immediately at the end of each class. Very often, pretending to be busy thinking and writing gradually leads to actually thinking and writing. There is no threat to any student at any level, because everyone can truly succeed. The writing is private and ungraded—only the teacher reviews it and then only holistically—but it "counts" (see Guidelines for a scoring guide). Advanced writers and thinkers don't have to worry about seeming "too smart" or "showing off," and those who are slower don't have to worry about seeming "too dumb" or being embarrassed. Requirements are specific: concrete thinking and writing about the student's personal experience with the assigned idea. It is the "assigned focus" (the Writing Project entry) and the expectation of immediate and active writing that makes the difference. Students learn what they do, and too often students haven't been doing anything.

With this method I talk less, but students write and then talk more. One of the rules of ecology is that it is impossible to do just one thing, and if we are not aware of this, we will inevitably cause harm. In education we should recognize this law and purposely do several things at once: observe and practice the rhetorical method or technique that is being studied for the out-of-class writing; learn about and connect to history, science, culture, ethics, or philosophy; recognize the humanity of the minds of the past and of our own minds; apply universal concerns to unique and personal points of view; practice writing with specific, concrete details and examples; experience varieties of style, organization, and development; engage in critical thinking.

What about copying the Writing Project entries and doing "drills"? Isn't this foolishly old-fashioned and a waste of time? No, it is both wise and a good use of time. One of the primary methods of human learning is copying—seeing, hearing, experiencing, absorbing, producing and reproducing. Whether it is in learning to speak, learning to drive, learning to work, learning to parent, or learning to write, the experience of copying causes skills to "rub off" on the learner. This is a kind of mentoring!

It is striking to note that in modern formal education we never use the copy method well or wisely. Too often we ask elementary students to copy things that are badly written or ridiculously thoughtless (being eight implies many things but not stupidity), and then when the student arrives at a higher grade level and is supposed to be able to read well, we switch everything to the book or the computer (plus a few worksheets). Clicking a mouse, joy-sticking around the screen, staring at a page, or filling in the blanks short-circuits direct engagement with the patterns of words and thoughts. Speed-reading may help gather information, but it will never help with reading or writing for meaning, expression, or precision. Students must *write* in order to learn to write, and in writing they need to use all their senses—tactile, aural, and visual: feeling the pen on the page or the fingers on the keys, saying the words silently or aloud as they write and revise, seeing the words gradually appear in order and patterns.

So here are my reasons for using the Writing Project Method in the classroom:

- It enables active and personal learning as well as interesting, challenging, and continuous practice.
- It encourages thinking and writing without overwhelming the teacher with work and correction.
- It creates immediate and concrete responses to specific ideas in writing and for discussion.
- It assumes students will be individually responsible for their thinking and learning.

This gradually leads to

- better study/work habits, including learning how to learn
- better attention in the class
- more personal involvement with the information and skills
- more concretely and specifically applied course content

I hope that *Writing from Life* will provide flexibility and freedom for you in both teaching and learning. It is carefully cross-referenced so that classroom work, reading assignments, and out-of-class writing can be less passive, less rigid, less detached, less pointless, and less conventional. Writing needs to become more connected and inspired, more easily tied to current events or unique local circumstances, more personal, more actively engaging, and more stimulating. If the classroom can bring the unique and the universal together in compelling ways, then both student and the "real world" will be healthier and more humane.

Writing from Life makes both teaching and learning more effective, more interesting, and more joyful. It is addressed to the self-learner that every student can be, one who is willing to explore and eager to discover. Each of us can only learn for ourselves, and ultimately everything rests on the student's choice. In this method there are no preconceived answers. The focus is on the learner's journey with the teacher as the guide and coach, and the journey is not a trivial one. Essays are important as tools to check progress on the path. Just as we demonstrate our progress in other skills by playing in the games, by singing the solo before the judge or audience, or by lifting the weight in the competition, so we must demonstrate skill in writing with the formal out-of-class essay. But the real goal is lifelong mindfulness, discovery, examination, and thoughtfulness.

I hope that *Writing from Life: Collecting and Connecting* enlivens and stimulates your teaching and learning, as it does mine.

Writing from Life: Collecting and Connecting

Text Plan

Preface (to the teacher)

How to Use This Book (to the student)
    Learning to Write:
        Writing is like learning a sport.
        Writing is like learning to make music.
        Writing is like weight training.
    A Perspective on Writing
    "The Watcher at the Gate" by Gail Godwin

Part One—A HUNDRED WRITING PROJECTS

Purpose of Using Writing Project Method:
    encouraging mental flexibility and endurance
    strengthening perception and analysis of values and ethics
    recording and examining the thought process
    examining choices and deciding
    exploring ideas, actions, and results
    exploring spontaneous, intuitive, imaginative writing

Part Two—SEEING: A COLLECTION OF READINGS

Purpose of reading with a writing course and of the choice of selections:
    encouraging alertness and mindfulness

    encouraging mental flexibility
    strengthening educational perception
    strengthening historical perception
    strengthening social perception
    strengthening scientific/environmental perception

Theme Focus: Perception and Thought
    Seeing Ignorance
    Seeing Metaphors
    Seeing Ourselves
    Seeing Others
    Seeing Nature
    Seeing the Past
    From Seeing to Persuading

Part Three—VISUALIZING ORGANIZATION:
        WAYS OF CONNECTING

Purpose of studying organization and rhetorical methods:
    sharpening perception of pattern and design
    strengthening focus and clarity
    encouraging reader-centered planning
    strengthening organization of developed and finished writing

Focus: Rhetorical Methods and Patterns of Organization
    Organizational Design
    Connections
    Describing
    Using Examples
    Narrating
    Classifying and Dividing
    Comparing and Contrasting
    Explaining a Process
    Explaining Cause and Effect
    Defining
    Arguing

APPENDIX:

Purpose: Learner assistance
    The Progress of an Essay: "The Mental Eye"
    Index of Authors and Titles
    Acknowledgments

Advantages of the Writing Project Method for Teaching Writing

1. The Writing Project Method creates constant, enforced skill practice in perception, thinking, and writing in intellectually manageable pieces. It allows excellent thinkers to work up to their potential, and it encourages inexperienced or poor thinkers to try.

2. The Writing Project Method reduces the sense of helplessness and failure for learners who have poor skills but active minds and also for learners with average skills and average minds. It is possible to fail only by stopping. Clearly visible effort to wrestle with the assigned idea in writing is the only requirement.

3. The Writing Project Method demands that learners focus on the topic at hand and act/do something productive in class. Learners cannot tune out of a class in which they have to individually produce writing that is due immediately.

4. The Writing Project Method encourages thinking about new ideas and about old ideas in new ways.

5. The Writing Project Method can be used at any intellectual and skill level for many reasons:

    - The projects are human questions and cannot be outgrown.
    - Seeing becomes more perceptive; thinking becomes more complex and more specific and concrete; writing becomes more skillful.
    - Learners at all levels of skill in all fields need to revisit and polish their ability to see, to think, and to communicate.
    - Growth should be encouraged, and so changes in thinking are expected from all levels of skill and intelligence.

    Modeling by the leader/coach can sometimes be both helpful and mutually interesting, especially for advanced classes. If the coach does an assignment as the students do it and shares it later *(after the students have had a chance to think and write their own thoughts)*, this illustrates that the questions/issues can and should be continually rethought by every "level" of thinker-writer. (It is essential that there be no preconceived "right answer" in any Writing Project.)

6. The Writing Project Method focuses learning for the most effective use of class time. The teacher/coach guides or directs thinking into productive channels and helps focus work so that learning is constant, incremental, and self-reinforcing. This method also helps

to prevent "the blind leading the blind" effect of vague peer analysis by increasing the efficiency and value of group discussion. Discussions work best or focus most clearly and usefully after time to think and write. The learner should not be encouraged to speak without thinking. Trading mutual thoughtlessness is rarely helpful.

7. The Writing Project Method encourages independent thought and analysis. It eliminates student fears of seeming "too serious" or "too smart" because the teacher/coach expects depth and insight, but does not put anyone on the spot. It reduces the negative effects of verbal first responses that often prevent other individuals (maybe less assertive, less imaginative, or less vocal, or also more reflective or more inventive) from thinking their own thoughts, or at least from making them known. It allows learners to have their own thoughts and to examine them without fear of peers or coach.

8. The Writing Project Method encourages connection to past thought. It reduces intellectual, ethical, and educational isolation. It encourages the writer to see himself or herself as part of the human intellectual stream, flowing from the past and into the future, constantly changing, yet constantly the same. It allows students to deal with universal issues in personally unique ways.

9. The Writing Project Method challenges the thinking process. It reduces automatic responses, clichés, and stereotypes. It encourages changes of point of view through reflection and analysis

10. The Writing Project Method encourages practice and increasing skill in critical thinking. (See Critical Thinking Checklist.)

11. The Writing Project Method encourages the habit of concrete, specific thought and writing using details and examples to show what the writer means. It reduces the habitual use of vague, generalized writing.

12. The Writing Project Method reduces teacher/coach overload. The student's entire Response Journal can be assessed either two or three times during the quarter/semester on a holistic basis with only a few words of encouragement, helpful observations, or constructive criticism written by the teacher/coach. A simple scoring guide can be devised for these responses. (See Guidelines.)

13. The Writing Project Method increases actual student writing, often by 100 to 200 percent, as compared to the number of words the would have written if the only writing experience was writing essays outside of class. Skills are learned by practice, and this includes the skill of writing.

14. The Writing Project Method can encourage multicultural understanding (depending on the ideas chosen by the teacher/coach).
15. The Writing Project Method encourages wrestling with ethical issues that grow out of scientific, political, social, or economic facts, situations, or conflicts.

How to Use the THINKING SKILLS CHECKLIST

This list of Thinking Skills can be copied and given to students at the beginning of the course as you explain the scope and purpose of critical thinking and the fact that *all writing is thinking*. Virtually every point can be tied into the writing process as we are studying it. Thinking Skills are directly connected to the Writing Project assignments in class, the exploratory writing that is done after an assigned reading out of class, and the formal theses, sentence outlines, and essays that are the primary focus of expository writing.

During the course, reference can be made back to specific critical thinking skills that are being used for Writing Projects or assignments. Continual referral to the list enables students to internalize critical thinking in all of its depth and breadth as an automatic part of every learning process.

The Thinking Skills list also demonstrates that even though certain skills may be natural or automatic to certain personality types, all of the skills can and should be taken into account. This helps students understand how other people think; for example, those who tend to emphasize facts can see how those who emphasize imagination are thinking. Students can also see that the entire repertoire of skills gives them a fuller and more balanced perspective.

The Thinking Skills list gives focus to the learning process. It shows how varied thought can be and how much of the thought process is actually being taught in writing courses. You may find that it also helps you, as a teacher, to focus your discussions more precisely so that reading, writing, and thinking are continually reinforcing each other.

THINKING SKILLS CHECKLIST

from the Minnesota Community College Teaching for Thinking Project

I. **THINKING CONCERNING THE FACTS**
   A. Factual clarity, accuracy, and fairness
   B. Observational detail, accuracy, and scope
   C. Effective record/recall strategies
   D. Pattern identification

II. **THINKING DRAWING ON IMAGINATION AND INSIGHT**
   A. Seeking the larger context
   B. Seeking alternative perspectives
   C. Relating the known to the unknown
   D. Seeking alternative means of expression
   E. Using questions as probes
   F. Applying learning to self-understanding
   G. Drawing lessons from experiences

III. **THINKING FOCUSED ON LOGIC AND ORDER**
   A. Identifying structure and order
   B. Identifying hierarchies
   C. Argument identification and evaluation
   D. Argument construction
   E. Rule manipulation
   F. Judging strength of evidence
   G. Awareness of thinking strategies (metacognition)

IV. **THINKING THAT BRINGS VALUES TO BEAR**
   A. Sensitivity to values—individual and collective
   B. Applying values to problems
   C. Respect for individual and collective differences
   D. Willingness to risk and commit
   E. Valuing your individual and collective self

Sample Syllabus

<u>ENGLISH COMPOSITION</u>   <u>5 quarter credits</u>
ENGLISH 121:04 **Tuesdays, CC;**
                Thursdays, #1301—9:00-10:50 A.M.
ENGLISH 121:05 **Wednesdays, #3940;**
                Fridays, CC—9:00-10:50 A.M.
Winter Quarter 1997—January 2-March 21
Phyllis Ballata, Century College—office #3454 West Campus
    phone and voice mail
Transfer and Academic Goal: Communication (5 qtr. cr.)

Texts: *Writing from Life: Collecting and Connecting*
          (Mayfield Publishing ISBN 1-55934-555-1)
          Century English Handbook, 6th edition

Class preparation:
Read/Writes:
1. Read the assignment.
2. Copy one seed or one other short quotation from each reading; record the author and source in correct bibliographic form.
3. Write a 250+ word personal response/reaction/meditation prompted by your chosen quotation and your reading. Compare and contrast your ideas and the ideas of the author. When using quotations from the source or other sources, use correct in-text citation form (See *Century English Handbook*).
4. Record the word count at the end.
5. Place the Read/Writes in your portfolio at the beginning of class on the day assigned.

Assignments should be done before coming to class.
Essays are always due at the *beginning* of class.

ASSIGNMENT SCHEDULE:
"Seeing"
1/2Th-3F   Course introduction—See *Writing from Life*,
            Introduction (1-4)
          Read/Write: The Watcher at the Gate (4-6)

1/7T-8W   Study Organization (375-379); Description
            (380-381); Example (382);
            Classification (384-385)
            Read/Write: Seeing (270-276)

1/9Th-10F	Read/Write: How Did We Come to This? (316-323) Read/Write: Ships in the Desert (324-327)
1/14T-15W	**Essay #1 due—Classification/Division: Advertisement Analysis** brainstorming, drafts with revisions, typed formal sentence outline, typed formal essay

"Seeing Metaphor"

1/16Th-17F	Study Comparison/Contrast (386-387) Read/Write: Hidden Teacher (167-169) Read/Write: Use (175-176)
1/21T-22W	Read/Write: The Crooked Tree (170) Read/Write: The Grand Tour (171-172)
1/23Th-24F	Read/Write: Icebergs and Cathedrals (177-179) Read/Write: Fire and Ice (180)
1/28T-29W	**Essay #2 due—Comparison/Contrast: An Extended Metaphor or Analogy** brainstorming, drafts with revisions, typed formal sentence outline, typed formal essay

"Seeing Others"

1/30Th-31F	Study Process (388-389); Narrative (383) Read/Write: The Grandmother (219) Read/Write: In Search of Our Mothers' Gardens (221-229)
2/4T-5W	Read/Write: Lullaby (240-247) Read Write: About Men (248-250)
2/6Th-7F	Read/Write: My Father (251-257) Read/Write: The Hired Man (258-260)
2/11T-12W	**Essay #3 due—Process Narrative: Another Person's Life Event** brainstorming, drafts with revisions, typed formal sentence outline, typed formal essay

"Seeing Ourselves"

2/13Th-14F	Study Cause/Effect (390-391) Read/Write: Theme for English B (181-182) Read/Write: Shame (183-186)

Part One: Theory, Organization, and Practical Information

2/18T-19W   Read/Write: How I Discovered Words (187-190)
            Read/Write: Naked to the Wolves (191-195)

2/20Th-21F Read/Write: The Canyon (196-200)
            Read/Write: Rain and the Rhinoceros (201-208)

2/25T-26W   **Essay #4 due—Cause/Effect:
               Thinking and Acting**
            brainstorming, drafts with revisions, typed
            formal sentence outline, typed formal essay

"From Seeing to Persuading"
2/27Th-28F Study Argument (393-394); Documentation
               (395-412)
            Read/Write: The Mental Eye
            Read/Write: I Like to Think of Harriet Tubman
               (335-337)

3/4T-5W   Read/Write: Scabies, Scrapie (338-341)
            Read/Write: The Clan of One-Breasted Women
               (328-334)

3/6Th-7F   Read/Write: Home of the Free (345-349)
            Read/Write: Industrial Tourism (350-358)
            TWO REVISIONS FROM ESSAYS #1-#4 DUE BY
               NOON MARCH 7 or before

3/11T-12W   **Essay #5 due—Argument: What do my
               choices do?
               (See Writing Project #98)**
            brainstorming, drafts with revisions, typed
            formal sentence outline, typed formal essay
            Study Definition (392)

3/13Th-14F READ/WRITES DUE BY NOON MARCH 14 or before
            **Essay #6—FINAL EXIT ESSAY—
               Extended Definition, written in
               class
               (See Writing Project #79)**
            Bring outline only.
            Pass/Fail for course. Any Final Exit Essay
            that Fails due to three or more major
            sentence errors (fragments, comma splices,
            run-ons) may be retaken during final week to
            attempt a Pass.

Final Week March 18T-21F
Quarter Break March 24-March 29
Spring Quarter March 31 to June 13

Refer to the *Century English Handbook* for questions about forms and general information for writing essays.

Attendance is expected. Absences of 10% of the class time or 4 hours are allowed for personal leave/sick leave without penalty. In-class writing can be done by asking for the Writing Projects and doing the work at home, in-class exercises can be done to some extent at home, lectures cannot be repeated but you may find someone to take notes. None of this will totally alleviate the problems that naturally come from being absent, but they will help somewhat.
Attendance includes 5 hours per week, including 10 hours in the Writing Center and 3 in individual conferences during the quarter.
"Writing Center Referrals" will be given with corrected essays. After you complete the work, the referral should be signed by the Writing Center Director or Professor and placed in my mailbox.

No one can learn for anyone else. Do your own reading, your own thinking, and your own writing and revising. Ask for help from whomever you wish, but do your own work and pay your own dues. No one learns any skill by expecting someone else to do the workouts, the practicing, or the final product.

We all learn to write by writing. There are many ways to practice this, but it is most important that you do your own thinking and writing. Even when you ask for help or ask for opinions from other people, make your thinking and writing your own work. WARNING: Plagiarism is using someone else's words or ideas without giving credit in an acceptable form (see *Century English Handbook*). It is stealing and will result in an F for the course.

Writing is a process, but the process should be completed when the work is submitted for assessment. Many drafts and revisions will create a quality finished essay. When the essay is due, it is handed in in finished form and graded as the carefully revised and finished document that it should be. Process is important, *but finished excellence is also important.*

Two revisions (from Essays #1-4) are part of the grading system so that you can incorporate suggested changes into your work. Essays #5 and #6 should demonstrate your final out-of-class and in-class writing skills.

GRADING:

Informal Exploratory Writing (200 points)
_____ 200 points total
   IN-CLASS exercises and drills + OUT-OF-CLASS Read/Writes
   Grading is holistic, emphasizing—
      (1) mental exercise
      (2) personal content compared or contrasted with others' ideas
      (3) specific and concrete writing
<u>Honors</u> (A-B) 90-100% of assignments and exercises are done
   Shows personal involvement with the assignment, care, attention to detail, and individual thought, especially including insight into the readings
<u>Satisfactory</u> (B-C) 80-90% of assignments and exercises are done
   Shows attention to the assignment, effort toward accomplishing the purpose, and some engagement with the ideas
<u>Unsatisfactory</u> (D-F) Less than 80% of the assignments and exercises are done
   Shows inattention, lack of effort, or little personal engagement

Formal Expository Writing (750 points)
750 points total—Grading emphasizes <u>both content and mechanics</u>:
   organization   focus
   specific/concrete development   fluency
   college-level writing facility and skills
_____100 pts. = Essay #1 — Classification (Advertisement Analysis)
_____100 pts. = Essay #2 — Comparison/Contrast (Extended Metaphor)
_____100 pts. = Essay #3 — Process Narrative (Life Event)
_____100 pts. = Essay #4 — Cause/Effect (Thinking and Acting)

Part One: Theory, Organization, and Practical Information   15

_____150 pts. = Essay #5 — Argument (What do my choices do?)
_____100 pts. = Essay #6 — Definition (final exit essay)
_____50 pts. = Revision #1 Rewritten/revised essays (from #1-4) with originals
_____50 pts. = Revision #2 holistic grading, no comments

Attendance (50 points)
_____50 pts total
0 absences = A+(5.3)   1-2 hours = A   3-4 hours = A-
5 hours = B   6 hours = C   7 hours = D
8 hours = F   More than 8 hours = drop from class

The grading point system

	A = 50	A- = 47	1000-901 points = A
B+ = 43	B = 40	B- = 37	900-701 points = B
C+ = 33	C = 30	C- = 27	700-501 points = C
D+ = 23	D = 20	D- = 17	500-301 points = D
	F = 10	0 = 0	300- = F

Qualities of a good essay
Organization
    clear, overall focus (thesis) (telling)
    unity (maintaining focus throughout)
    clear subpoints (topic sentences) (telling)
    useful and effective paragraph divisions
    closure
Content
    carefully designed and developed support for each
        point (showing)
    selection of specific, concrete details and
        examples (showing)
    thoughtful discussion of ideas
Mechanics
    correct use of standard English
Fluency
    coherence (sticking togetherness)
    flows smoothly from paragraph to paragraph,
        sentence to sentence, idea to idea
Word Choice
    accurate in meaning and tone
    fitting for the audience and writing situation
Originality
    sense of personal voice
    fresh or new or imaginative perspective

16   Part One: Theory, Organization, and Practical Information

EXPLORATORY WRITING RECORD

Out-of-class explorations	In-class explorations and drills
Read/Writes, 250+ words each	Timed in class
Watcher at the Gate (4-6)	1.
Seeing (270-276)	2.
How Did We Come to This? (316-323)	3.
Ships in the Desert (324-327)	4.
The Hidden Teacher (167-169)	5.
Use (175-176)	6.
The Crooked Tree (170)	7.
The Grand Tour (171-172)	8.
Icebergs and Cathedrals (177-179)	9.
Fire and Ice (180)	10.
The Grandmother (219)	11.
In Search of Our Mothers' Gardens (221-229) 12.	12.
Lullaby (240-247)	13.
About Men (248-250)	14.
My Father (251-257)	15.
The Hired Man (258-260)	16.
Theme for English B (181-182)	17.
Shame (183-186)	18.
How I Discovered Words (187-190)	19.
Naked to the Wolves (191-195)	20.
The Canyon (196-200)	21.
Rain and the Rhinoceros (201-208)	22.
The Mental Eye	23.

Part One: Theory, Organization, and Practical Information 17

I Like to Think of Harriet Tubman (335-337)
Scabies, Scrapie (338-341)
The Clan of One-Breasted Women (328-334)
Home of the Free (345-349)
Industrial Tourism (350-358)

24.
25.
26.
27.
28.
29.
30.
31.
32.
33.
34.
35.

WRITING CENTER REFERRAL FOR _____ Date _____

After reading information handouts or handbooks on this subject, complete at least one worksheet to test your understanding of the skills. Correct it yourself. Ask the Writing Center Director or the professor on duty to explain anything you do not understand. You need to eliminate this problem from your future work and/or understand the issue more clearly for future reference.

Writing Center Handouts and Worksheets

Subjects
Elements of a Sentence
Subject-Verb-Direct Object
Subject-Verb-Indirect
    Object-Direct Object
Conjunctions
Adverb Clauses
Noun Clauses
Fragments
Subject Verb Agreement
Misplaced Modifiers
Punctuation

Verbs
Subject-Verb
Subject-Verb-Subject
    Complement
Prepositions
Clauses
Adjective Clauses
Gerunds
Comma Splices/Run-on
    Sentences
Adjectives & Adverbs
Pronouns
MLA Style Sheet

Issues in Handbooks—

Formal Sentence Outlines
Rhetorical Methods
Clearness
Wordiness
Paragraphing
Introductions

Thesis Statements
Idiomatic Language
Specific, Concrete
    Development
Topic Sentences
Order of Development
Conclusions

Other: _____

Comments:

Attach the completed worksheet(s).

_____
sign, Writing Center Director

_____
sign, Student

Sample Writing Projects

See Syllabus for assignments.

These are designed for a two-hour class period, but they can easily be adapted to one-hour blocks of time.

It usually takes about 10–15 minutes of introduction and discussion to focus the Project specifically on the practice idea at hand. Most in-class Writing Projects are timed at 10 to 15 minutes for writing.

#1 Essay preparation (#1)

   Practice with advertisements provided in class.
   1. Describe the advertisement in detail.
   2. Focus on facts and their meanings: ex., color, image, design, etc.
   3. Focus on the messages, conscious and unconscious; consider the producer, the advertiser, the reader, the buyer.
   4. Focus on the psychology of the ad.

#2 Using your own ad

   [after a discussion of specific and concrete, page 380]
   Create a list of *specific* description and examples.
   Create a list of *concrete* description and examples.

#3 Write a thesis and some subpoints for paragraphs in outline form
   [after a discussion of organizational design, pages 377–378].

#4 On Seeing—Writing Project 21
   Describe the last hour using specific, concrete details and examples.

#5 Aims of Advertising—Writing Project 57
   Use the advertisement for your essay.
   Do as many parts of the Writing Project as you have time for:
   What fears, anxieties, desires, etc. does the ad create in you?
   Who is the target audience and what are they supposed to be like?
   Are you the target audience? What is your reaction?

#6   Drill—page 316, paragraph 5 from "How Did We Come to This?"

Copy exactly as written. Pay special attention to vocabulary, sentence construction, punctuation, and paragraph construction (topic sentence and development).

#7   On Day and Night—Writing Project 30

Describe night using specific, concrete details and examples in similes and metaphors.

#8   Color—Writing Project 31

Describe a color using specific, concrete details and examples in similes and metaphors.

#9   Drill—page 317, paragraph 10 from "How Did We Come to This?"

Copy exactly as written. Pay attention to vocabulary, sentence construction, punctuation, and paragraph construction (topic sentence and development).

#10   Facts versus Interpretation—Writing Project 51

Explain the metaphor comparing thoughtless economic growth with cancer: "Growth for the sake of growth is cancerous madness" (Abbey 66).

First list the characteristics of cancer; then make a parallel list of possible characteristics of "growth for the sake of growth" in urban and economic development that Abbey might be considering.

#11   On Reading—Writing Project 55

Examine the metaphor "These are not books, lumps of lifeless paper, but minds alive on the shelves. From each of them goes out its own voice . . ." (Highet 71) using the short story "Use" by Griffin (175–176) as the "mind."

#12   Essay Preparation (#2)

Using your own idea for comparing a concept that you understand or a skill that you know how to do to something else that the rest of us would recognize, work out the analogy or extended comparison

1. Make an equation: X is like Y
2. Match the characteristics of the two concepts or skills (X and Y)
3. Brainstorm by writing sample paragraphs

Samples from the Readings:

"The Hidden Teacher":

Man's relation to his universe is like a spider's relation to its universe (web).

Man's relation to his universe is like blood cells' relation to their universe (the body).

Uncontrolled urban growth is like cancer. (Abbey #51)

A book's message is like the radio waves in this room. (Highet #55)

"Introduction"

Learning to write is like learning a sport.

Learning to write is like learning to make music.

Learning to write is like weight training.

"The Crooked Tree"

This crooked tree is like your teaching.

"The Grand Tour"

The roadside ditch at night is like a bazaar.

The roadside ditch at night is like a church service in a right-wing dictatorship.

#13   Knowing One's Self—Writing Project 62

Explain the metaphor (comparison) in this poem (I am like an iceberg).

#14   Drill—page 225, paragraph 29 from "In Search of Our Mothers' Gardens"

Copy exactly; use the correct in-text citation and make a correct bibliographic entry.

#15   Are You Raw or Cooked?—Writing Project 73b

Illustrate the difference between familiarity with contempt and familiarity with respect. Discuss the process of understanding someone else and the issue of respect by using examples from your life.

22   Part One: Theory, Organization, and Practical Information

#16 On Grief—Writing Project 3a/b

Write a *first-person* narrative about a time when either

a. others did not know of or understand your problem and so did not respond in a helpful way, *or*

b. you did not know about another's problem and so you could not grieve with him or her or understand how he or she felt.

#17 Drill—page 249, paragraph 3 from "About Men"

Copy exactly; pay attention to style, tone, fluency, rhythm, focus, use of details and examples.

#18 On Growing Old—Writing Project 78

Write a *third-person* process narrative explaining "growing old." Consider the realities and the ideals that you are personally familiar with, but be sure that your discussion uses third person grammatical point of view.

#19 Essay Preparation (#3)

Brainstorm for details for your third-person process narrative about someone else. Either list details, then rearrange in chronological order and then into groupings for paragraphs, or list questions you need to ask about the event.

#20 Drill—pages 251–52, paragraph 6 from "My Father's Life"

Copy exactly, noticing sentence construction, vocabulary, style, tone, rhythm, voice, and fluency.

#21 The Value of Mistakes—Writing Project 14d

Decide whether you agree or disagree with Leopold in some specific case. Prove your point by writing a narrative to *show* what you think.

#22 Preparing for Good Luck—Writing Project 59

Causes and effects are related in complicated ways. Sometimes we need to decide what we want the "effect" to be before we can make the "cause" happen. Our thoughts lead to our actions in this case.

What *effect* (result) are you preparing for? What skills are you now creating that may *cause* this *effect* to be possible?

After:

Make a "cartoon" or "map" of your idea using the methods on pages 390–391.

Make a topic outline (basic order).

Make a sentence outline (order + direction and focus).

#23 Drill—page 183, paragraph 3 from "Shame"

Copy exactly; make a correct in-text citation and bibliographic entry.

After:

Notice the punctuation (or lack of it) in sentence 2. Adding punctuation to a quotation means using brackets: [ ]. Add commas after the dependent clauses and before the "and" in compound constructions in order to see how punctuation helps the reading.

"When I played the drums in high school[,] it was for Helene[,] and when I broke track records in college[,] it was for Helene[,] and when I started standing behind microphones and heard applause[,] I wished Helene could hear it, too" (Gregory 183).

#24 Means and Ends—Writing Project 67b

Thinking about the goal you considered in #22, what do you still have to learn in order to achieve your aim? What understanding, values, attitudes, ideas, skills, and/or talents do you still need to develop that will cause your goal to be reached?

#25 Essay preparation (#4)

After a discussion with your group, brainstorm for 5 to 10 minutes and then make a map of your plan.

#26 Being Alone—Writing Project 61b

What are the results (effects) of too much time alone?

or

What are the results (effects) of not enough time alone?

#27 Drill—page 194, paragraph 29 from "Naked to the Wolves"

Copy exactly. Make a correct in-text citation and bibliographic entry.

#28 Preventing Problems in the First Place—Writing Project 33

Analyze the causes of a recent (small) problem you have had.

Explain how the problem came to happen.

After:

Discuss the ways you could have prevented it by foreseeing this cause-effect relationship.

#29   Essay/conference preparation (#4)

Draw a map of your essay as it actually is.

Bring this map and your draft to your conference.

#30   Are We Tools of Our Tools?—Writing Project 10d

If you "vote" with your dollars, what does your money say? What do your spending habits show that you value, think is important, or think is right?

#31   What Do We Owe Future Generations?—Writing Project 13b

Using your "votes" from #30, how do your choices affect future generations?

Argue for or against personally caring about this.

#32   What Do Your Choices Do?—Writing Project 98 (Essay preparation #5)

Using one of the choices from #30 or #31, write a paragraph explaining the effects of your choice in the world right now. Then argue for or against this particular choice.

#33   And Who Is My Neighbor?—Writing Project #88

88a—Answer the question "Who is my neighbor?"

88c—Argue for or against the proposition that business should be based on neighborliness and good character, using practical, "real-world" considerations.

#34   Wasting the Body, Wasting the Spirit—Writing Project 85a–e

Argue for or against one of Berry's propositions.

#35   What Is Happiness?—Writing Project 66c

Argue for or against Merton's proposition that happiness depends on "the ability to get away from ourselves, and our own limited sphere of interests and appetites and needs." Use specific, concrete details and examples to support your position.

#36 The Value of Limits—Writing Project 29a

Choose one of the "limits" on your personal freedom, wishes, actions, emotions, or choices that you accept. Argue for this limit by considering the advantages *and disadvantages* of the limitation, explaining why you personally accept it.

#37 What Is Happiness?—Writing Project 66a

Write your personal definition of happiness.

#38 Sin and Virtue—Writing Project 79a–c (Essay preparation #6)

Pick *one* of the Seven Deadly Sins or the Four Cardinal Virtues and brainstorm for ideas. Prepare to write an extended definition essay in class during the next class period. [This is for the Exit Essay.]

Drills

Drills are copy-observation exercises. Just like inviting the "star" to come in person to demonstrate for the hopeful amateur, drills invite the master writer to demonstrate writing for the student of writing. The student copies a passage exactly, usually a paragraph unit of about 100 words, in order to examine firsthand how the master writer uses focus; specific, concrete development; vocabulary; rhythm; sentence construction; punctuation; tone; and voice to create his or her style and to communicate ideas.

Drills can be chosen to illustrate specific issues, such as design of topic sentences and paragraph development; use of specific or concrete details and examples; control of tone through vocabulary or sentence construction, stylistic devices, or fluency. Drills are often chosen from readings that students have recently been assigned or from those to be assigned in the next day or two. This helps connect out-of-class and in-class work.

Sample Drills from *Writing from Life*, "Part Two: Seeing: A Collection of Readings"

Seeing Ignorance:
Kerwin—page 135, paragraph 32; page 140, paragraph 67; page 141, paragraph 71
Thomas—page 145, paragraph 4; page 147, paragraph 11
Gould—page 149, paragraph 2
Ferris—page 153, paragraph 4 (including quote); page 156, paragraph 15

Carson—page 159, paragraph 3
Beston—page 162, paragraph 2
Raymo—page 164, paragraph 2

Seeing Metaphors:
Eiseley—page 167, paragraph 3; page 168, paragraph 7
Holm—page 171, paragraph 2
Lopez—pages 178–179, paragraph 11

Seeing Ourselves:
Gregory—page 183, paragraph 3
Malcolm X—page 189, paragraph 18
Mowat—pages 192–193, paragraph 16; page 194, paragraph 29
Abbey—page 196, paragraph 1; page 199, paragraph 23
Merton—page 201, paragraph 1; page 202, paragraph 8; pages 206–207, paragraph 34
Ozick—page 209, paragraph 1
Didion—page 213, paragraph 6

Seeing Others:
Walker—page 222, paragraph 12; page 225, paragraph 29; page 226, paragraph 38; page 228, paragraph 48
Kingston—page 238, paragraph 49
Silko—page 240, paragraph 3
Ehrlich—page 249, paragraph 3
Carver—pages 251–252, paragraph 6; page 256, paragraph 30

Seeing Nature:
Holm—page 265, paragraph 6; page 266, paragraph 8
Dillard—page 272, paragraph 7
Leopold—page 277, paragraph 3
Rupp—page 279, paragraph 4; page 280, paragraph 8
Eiseley—page 284, paragraph 1

Seeing the Past:
Lopez—page 290, paragraph 5
Momaday—page 299, paragraph 17
Leopold—page 314, paragraph 52

Gordon and Suzuki—page 316, paragraph 5; page 317, paragraph 10

Gore—page 324, paragraph 1

Williams—page 329, paragraph 20

From Seeing to Persuading:

Thomas—page 339, paragraph 5

Morowitz—page 342, paragraph 1; pages 342–343, paragraph 4

Berry—page 346, paragraph 6; page 347, paragraph 11

Abbey—page 351, paragraph 8; pages 352–353, paragraph 14; page 356, paragraph 30

Deloria—pages 360–361, paragraph 12; page 363, paragraph 26; page 365, paragraph 37

Schumacher—page 368, paragraph 7; page 370, paragraph 14

Lesson Plan Chart

In order to keep track of both future plans and past work, a quarter- or semester-length lesson plan chart is very helpful.

1. A lesson plan chart enables the teacher to plan the sequence of assignments and in-class practice sessions specifically to contribute to the students' understanding of their out-of-class writing and to systematically cover all of the required material for the course.

2. The lesson record makes giving makeup work easier and more efficient.

3. The lesson record simplifies planning for future quarters and semesters because not only are the Writing Projects and the discussion topics in one convenient place, but so are comments about what changes to consider and which Projects or discussions worked the best.

SAMPLE LESSON PLAN CHART

Date _____

Out-of-class preparation assigned for today (reading/writing)

General work to be done in class, or lecture topic

Writing Project numbers, letters, and directions for in-class writing

Variations or additions to Writing Project wording for later use or for makeup work

Comments/Notes from teacher to himself or herself

Record Chart for _____ (quarter/semester) _____ (year)

Date

Student preparation

Class work

Writing Projects

Variations?

Comments

Date

Student preparation

Class work

Writing Projects

Variations?

Comments

Date

Student preparation

Class work

Writing Projects

Variations?

Comments

Alternative Syllabi Ideas

Rhetorical/Expository Method class design: (see Sample Syllabus and Reference Charts in Part Two)

Theme class designs:
Seeing/perception (the controlling theme of the text)

1. Seeing Ignorance
    —recognizing, accepting, and using ignorance
    —recognizing the role of ignorance in learning and education

2. Seeing Metaphors
    —recognizing and understanding how thinkers use metaphors
    —discovering and using metaphor to explain and clarify ideas

3. Seeing Ourselves
    —seeing and understanding ourselves as individuals
    —recognizing strengths and weaknesses in thought processes, points of view, and individual personalities

4. Seeing Others
    —seeing and understanding others as individuals
    —recognizing the importance of context and subtext

5. Seeing Nature
    —seeing and understanding nature
    —recognizing the interaction between facts and interpretations
    —recognizing the importance of active perception, intellectual analysis, and emotional response

6. Seeing the Past
    —seeing and understanding the facts and interpretations of the past
    —recognizing the importance of political, economic, social, and psychological context
    —connecting the past and the present

Part One: Theory, Organization, and Practical Information   31

7. From Seeing to Persuading
   —seeing and thinking about contro-versial issues, then persuading others
   —recognizing the influence of analysis, reflection, and judgment on point of view
   —recognizing the influence of context and subtext on personal opinion
   —recognizing the importance of logic, proof, reasoning, and emotion in argument

Readings for Theme Class Designs

Gender

"The Grandmother," "In Search of Our Mothers' Gardens," "No Name Woman," "Lullaby," "About Men," "My Father's Life," "I Like to Think of Harriet Tubman," "Use," "The Clan of One-Breasted Women," "Scabies, Scrapie," "Women's Lib and the Battle Against Entropy"

Law and Justice

"The Grand Tour," "Shame," "How I Discovered Words," "Rain and the Rhinoceros," "In Search of Our Mothers' Gardens," "No Name Woman," "Lullaby," "The Death of the Hired Man," "The Sparrow Hawk," "Ozymandias," "The Passing Wisdom of Birds," "The Way to Rainy Mountain," "Good Oak," "How Did We Come to This?" "Ships in the Desert," "The Clan of One-Breasted Women," "I Like to Think of Harriet Tubman," "Industrial Tourism"

Individual and Community

"The Anatomy of Ignorance," "Humanities and Science," "The Sense of Wonder," "Birds," "The Hidden Teacher," "The Crooked Tree," "The Grand Tour," "Agricultural Solutions for Agricultural Problems," "Fire and Ice," "Theme for English B," "Shame," "How I Discovered Words," "Rain and the Rhinoceros," "In Search of Our Mothers' Gardens," "No Name Woman," "Lullaby," "The Death of the Hired Man," "Ozymandias," "The Passing Wisdom of Birds," "The Way to Rainy Mountain," "Good Oak," "How Did We Come to This?" "Ships in the Desert," "The Clan of One-Breasted Women," "I Like to Think of Harriet Tubman," "Women's Lib and the Battle Against Entropy," "Home of the Free," "Industrial Tourism," "Buddhist Economics"

Ethics

"The Persistence of Mystery," "The Crooked Tree," "The Grand Tour," "Use," "Shame," "Rain and the Rhinoceros," "In Search of Our Mothers' Gardens," "No Name Woman," "Lullaby," "My Father's Life," "The Death of the Hired Man," "The Sparrow Hawk," "Ozymandias," "The Passing Wisdom of Birds," "A White Heron," "Good Oak," "How Did We Come to This?" "Ships in the Desert," "The Clan of One-Breasted Women," "I Like to Think of Harriet Tubman," "Women's Lib and the Battle Against Entropy," "Home of the Free," "Industrial Tourism," "We Talk, You Listen," "Buddhist Economics"

Medicine

"Use," "Lullaby," "My Father's Life," "The Death of the Hired Man," "Two Ways of Seeing the River," "How Did We Come to This?" "Ships in the Desert," "The Clan of One-Breasted Women," "Scabies, Scrapie," "Home of the Free"

Agriculture

"The Crooked Tree," "The Grand Tour," "Agricultural Solutions for Agricultural Problems," "Use," "The Grandmother," "In Search of Our Mothers' Gardens," "No Name Woman," "Lullaby," "About Men," "The Death of the Hired Man," "Horizontal Grandeur," "Good Oak," "How Did We Come to This?" "Ships in the Desert," "Home of the Free," "Buddhist Economics"

Education

"The Anatomy of Ignorance," "Humanities and Science," "Darwin's Middle Road," "The Persistence of Mystery," "The Sense of Wonder," "The Hidden Teacher," "The Crooked Tree," "Agricultural Solutions for Agricultural Problems," "Use," "Icebergs and Cathedrals," "Theme for English B," "Shame," "How I Discovered Words," "Naked to the Wolves," "Rain and the Rhinoceros," "The Seam of the Snail," "On Keeping a Notebook," "In Search of Our Mothers' Gardens," "Lullaby," "My Father's Life," "The Death of the Hired Man," "Horizontal Grandeur," "The Forest," "Seeing," "The Deer Swath," "Knowing the Names," "Two Ways of Seeing the River," "The Sparrow Hawk," "A White Heron," "Good Oak," How Did We Come to This?" "Ships in the Desert," "The Clan of One-Breasted Women," "I Like to Think of Harriet Tubman," "Scabies, Scrapie," "Home of the Free," "We Talk, You Listen," "Buddhist Economics"

Other examples of themes
    human relationships
    social issues
    environmental issues
    specific historical or philosophical points of view
    multicultural points of view

Academic Discipline class design:

Behavioral Sciences

(anthropology, political science, psychology, sociology)

"The Anatomy of Ignorance," "Humanities and Science," "The Grand Tour," "Use," "Theme for English B," "Shame," "How I Discovered Words," "Naked to the Wolves," "Rain and the Rhinoceros," "The Seam of the Snail," "On Keeping a Notebook," "The Grandmother," "In Search of Our Mothers' Gardens," "No Name Woman," "Lullaby," "About Men," "My Father's Life," "The Death of the Hired Man," "Horizontal Grandeur," "Ozymandias," "The Passing Wisdom of Birds," "The Way to Rainy Mountain," "A White Heron," "Good Oak," "How Did We Come to This?" "Ships in the Desert," "The Clan of One-Breasted Women," "I Like to Think of Harriet Tubman," "Home of the Free," "We Talk, You Listen," "Buddhist Economics"

Science and Technology

"Humanities and Science," "Darwin's Middle Road," "The Persistence of Mystery," "The Sense of Wonder," "Birds," "The Silence," "The Hidden Teacher," "Use," "Icebergs and Cathedrals," "Naked to the Wolves," "Rain and the Rhinoceros," "A White Heron," "Good Oak," "How Did We Come to This?" "Ships in the Desert," "The Clan of One-Breasted Women," "Buddhist Economics"

History

"The Anatomy of Ignorance," "Darwin's Middle Road," "Agricultural Solutions to Agricultural Problems," "Use," "Icebergs and Cathedrals," "In Search of Our Mothers' Gardens," "No Name Woman," "Lullaby," "My Father's Life," "Horizontal Grandeur," "Ozymandias," "A White Heron," "The Passing Wisdom of Birds," "The Way to Rainy Mountain," "Good Oak," "How Did We Come to This?" "Ships in the Desert," "The Clan of One-Breasted Women," "I Like to Think of Harriet Tubman," "We Talk, You Listen," "Buddhist Economics"

Literature

Poetry: "What the Dog Perhaps Hears," "Fire and Ice," "Theme for English B," "The Grandmother," "The Death of the Hired Man," "To Make a Prairie," "Oh, Lovely Rock," "Ozymandias," "I Like to Think of Harriet Tubman"

Stories: "The Crooked Tree," "Use," "No Name Woman," "Lullaby," "A White Heron"

Economics and Politics

"Use," "Shame," "Rain and the Rhinoceros," "Horizontal Grandeur," "Ozymandias," "The Passing Wisdom of Birds," "A White Heron," "Good Oak," "How Did We Come to This?" "Ships in the Desert," "The Clan of One-Breasted Women," "Scabies, Scrapie," "Home of the Free," "Buddhist Economics"

Cultures

"The Crooked Tree," "Theme for English B," "Naked to the Wolves," "The Canyon," "The Grandmother," "In Search of Our Mothers' Gardens," "No Name Woman," "Lullaby," "The Passing Wisdom of Birds," "The Way to Rainy Mountain," "We Talk, You Listen," "Buddhist Economics"

Issues and Controversies class design:

—Social and historical issues in readings and Writing Projects include, for example:

totalitarianism, literacy, right use, mechanism, conquest, Native American identity and rights, attitudes toward nature, agriculture vs. agribusiness, environmental degradation, nuclear testing, stewardship, medical technology, death and dying, law, poverty, attitudes toward women, patriarchy, freedom, education, elitism, recreation, mass media, gardening, limitation, religion, business, economics

Classroom Guidelines

Grading (see also: Sample Scoring guide)

A writing course is a skill class, and the grade is based overwhelmingly on writing skills.

The relative grade breakdown I generally use with a rhetorical method organization in a first-level freshman expository essay class is 20 percent for Informal Exploratory Writing (Journal for Writing Projects and Reading

Responses), 75 percent for Formal Expository Writing, and 5 percent for Attendance and Participation. At my college there is no extensively researched paper at this first level of freshman composition (although documentation is introduced); research is done in the second-level freshman composition class. (This text can also be used in that level.)

Sample of Grading Using a Percentage System

90% writing; 10% attendance and participation (other than writing):

20%	Journal: In-class and out-of-class Responses (emphasizes specific, concrete details and examples)
10%	Classification
10%	Comparison/Contrast
10%	Process
10%	Cause/Effect
20%	Persuasion (Final out-of-class Essay)
10%	Final in-class Exit Essay—Definition
10%	Attendance and class participation

Sample of Grading Using a Point System: 1,000 points total

Informal Exploratory Writing (200 points)
In-class Writing Projects and out-of-class Reading Responses

Formal Expository Writing (750 points)
100 points Essay #1
100 points Essay #2
100 points Essay #3
100 points Essay #4
50 points Revision #1
50 points Revision #2
150 points Essay #5—Final out-of-class Essay
100 points Essay #6—Final in-class Exit Essay

Attendance and Class Participation (50 points)

Timing

Writing Projects in class need to be timed carefully. They should be long enough to get beyond the first gush and froth of ideas and into something more substantial and specific, but short enough so that almost everyone can keep going without losing focus or attention.

Writing Project entries are focused for exploring thoughts and experiences and for experimenting with thought patterns (rhetorical methods). They should be imaginative, intuitive writing to discover where the focus will take the writer and to find new methods of thinking. One of the ways to fend off "the Watcher at the Gate" is to write *under* pressure but *without* pressure! In other words, the writer knows that the end is in sight (this will not go on forever) and that the only requirement is thought about the focus (no neatness other than readability, no grammar checks, no spelling checks, etc.). The writer can even change his or her mind in midstream.

In my experience, about 15 minutes of writing time is both long enough and short enough to accomplish these goals. This can, of course, be arranged according to the needs of the class and the idea itself.

The teacher/coach should pay attention to the class during this writing time. The students will sense if the teacher/coach is distracted or unaware of each of them or using the time to correct papers or do "chores." Doing this to the class is disrespectful. If this is worth the students' time, then it is worth the teacher/coach's attention.

Discussion

Discussions are greatly improved by the addition of time to think and write beforehand in the students' Response Journals.

In discussions of reading from *Writing from Life*, students can write out-of-class preparation entries using specific Seeds (listed after the assigned reading) or using any quotation they wish to consider from that reading. Writing a Response Journal entry that they must focus themselves based on their reading and thinking is helpful to them individually and to the class discussions as a whole. If the class has a number of immature members, these out-of-class preparation assignments can be placed in their Response Journals at the beginning of class. The students will remember what they wrote, but they will not (and should not) be writing the out-of-class preparation assignments during a discussion.

In discussions of ideas from *Writing from Life*, students can explore what they think as individuals before engaging in group discussions. A Writing Project assignment can be introduced (10 minutes); students can write (10–15 minutes); a small and then large group discussion can take place (10–15 minutes); and then students can write again (5 minutes), if the teacher chooses, all within a 50-minute class. This means that even the shyest people will have something to say and that compulsive talkers will have to share the time. When more writing is done after a discussion, students can rethink their responses based on talking it out. Students need to know that they are expected (allowed, encouraged) to change or develop their thoughts gradually through thinking, writing, and discussing. A thought process is never "finished" as long as new life experiences continue.

Practical Arrangements for Keeping Response Journals and Writing Projects

Copying is an age-old method of human learning that involves visual, aural, and tactile learning styles—seeing, saying, feeling the words and patterns. Copying the words of a master writer is an important part of the Writing Project Method (see "A Letter to Colleagues"). *Writing from Life* makes this simple for both the student and the teacher. Without the text, students have to copy from the board or overhead—unnecessarily difficult for all and almost impossible for some.

Many modern students have never experienced copying a master writer as a learning method, and they have never been actually, physically involved with close observation of the words on a page. It seems to me that this is one reason why so many write so poorly. Copying means paying attention to detail, to the sound and sense and sight of the words, to the design and organization of thought patterns, to the style and tone of the writer's voice, to the exact vocabulary choices, to the construction and punctuation of the sentences that create meaning. Both the teacher and the student must allow this kind of organic learning to happen—it will be worth the effort and the time it takes. Reading and experience are important for developing writing skill, but for many students both seeing and reading have become almost entirely passive. A "feel" for writing still requires reading, writing practice, and time, but it is greatly enhanced by a more active reading-copy-writing method.

The readings in *Writing from Life* and the entries in "A Hundred Writing Projects" are chosen from a variety of styles and voices. In order to stimulate thought and to encourage mental flexibility, these are deliberately different from the commonly available styles and voices found in the mass media and popular culture. In developing his or her own voice, the student must see and hear many of the interesting and acceptable kinds of styles and voices that are used by master writers. Active involvement with the reproduction and production of words and ideas is most helpful for all writers at all levels.

In my writing class, Response Journals are used in the classroom, and any out-of-class preparation assignments can be brought to class and added to the student's file. Therefore, I bring the Response Journal files to and from class every day and keep them together until the end of the term.

I prefer a simple two-pocket folder for each student. The students place their writing (numbered and dated, stapled if necessary) into this file at the end of each writing class: one pocket for in-class Writing Projects and one pocket for out-of-class Reading Responses. Makeup work can be done outside of class and brought in for the file. Because the files are always in my possession, I can "grade" them any time I choose. I usually use the inside of the folder for my comments and grade record.

Makeup work can be done outside of class using the Writing Project ideas and specific assignments. *Writing from Life* makes this very simple because it allows the teacher to keep track of assignments by number and letter in his or her lesson records for the quarter or semester. (See the Record Chart.) I let students be responsible. Doing makeup work is their problem, not mine. In my classes, Response Journal work must be done to be eligible for an A.

Sample Scoring Guide Using Letter Grades

Points	Criteria
1	Response entry (correct and complete entry, including author and source)
1	Focus (on assignment)
1	Development of discussion (specific, concrete details and/or examples)
1	Thinking process (effort to deal with complexity, implications, and/or actions)
____	Total 0 = F; 1 = D; 2 = C; 3 = B; 4 = A

Sample Scoring Guide Using Holistic Marking

+	honors, well developed and focused; correct length in words or in proportion for time allowed
√	OK, some attempt to deal with the ideas and focus; borderline/minimum length in words or time proportion
short	specific marking for out-of-class responses fewer than 250 words, but otherwise good or OK
0	not done, no credit

PART TWO
REFERENCE CHARTS

WRITING PROJECTS REFERENCE CHARTS

Number and Title

Authors

Key Ideas

Rhetorical Methods

See also (connections to readings)

Comments

1. **Collecting and Connecting**

Author: Ralph Waldo Emerson

Key ideas: History and its connection to personal experience and thought; history as biography

Rhetorical methods: comparison/contrast, narration, example, analysis, argument

See also: Shelley, "Ozymandias"; Lopez, "The Passing Wisdom of Birds"; Gore, "Ships in the Desert"; Griffin, "Use"; Lopez, "Icebergs and Cathedrals"; Walker, "In Search of Our Mothers' Gardens"; Kingston, "No Name Woman"; Silko, "Lullaby"; Momaday, "The Way to Rainy Mountain"; Leopold, "Good Oak"; Williams, "The Clan of One-Breasted Women"; Griffin, "I Like to Think of Harriet Tubman"; Deloria, "We Talk, You Listen"

Comments:

2. **What Is Education?**

Author: Aldo Leopold

Key ideas: education, awareness, the trade-offs in specialization

Rhetorical methods: definition, example, cause/effect, process

See also: Twain, "Two Ways of Seeing the River"; Jewett, "A White Heron"; Kerwin, "The Anatomy of Ignorance"; Thomas, "Humanities and Science"; Carson, "The Sense of Wonder"; Berry, "Agricultural Solutions for Agricultural Problems"; Hughes, "Theme for English B"; Gregory, "Shame"; Malcolm X, "How I

Discovered Words"; Ozick, "The Seam of the Snail"; Silko, "Lullaby"; Frost, "The Death of the Hired Man"; Rupp, "Knowing the Names"; Thomas, "Scabies, Scrapie"

Comments:

3. **On Grief**

Author: Aldo Leopold

Key ideas: the connection between grief and knowledge; "world of wounds"; tragedy versus history

Rhetorical methods: example, narration, cause/effect, process, analysis

See also: Gordon and Suzuki, "How Did We Come to This?"; Gore, "Ships in the Desert"; Williams, "The Clan of One-Breasted Women"; Griffin, "Use"; Gregory, "Shame"; Walker, "In Search of Our Mothers' Gardens"; Kingston, "No Name Woman"; Silko, "Lullaby"; Carver, "My Father's Life"; Frost, "The Death of the Hired Man"; Lopez, "The Passing Wisdom of Birds"; Griffin, "I Like to Think of Harriet Tubman"; Deloria, "We Talk, You Listen"

Comments:

4. **"What You See Is What You Get"**

Author: Annie Dillard

Key ideas: seeing versus not seeing; perception and understanding

Rhetorical methods: comparison/contrast, example, process, definition

See also: Dillard, "Seeing"; Ferris, "The Persistence of Mystery"; Kerwin, "The Anatomy of Ignorance"; Beston, "Birds"; Mueller, "What the Dog Perhaps Hears"; Eiseley, "The Hidden Teacher"; Hoff, "The Crooked Tree"; Ozick, "The Seam of the Snail"; Thoreau, "The Forest"; Leopold, "The Deer Swath"; Rupp, "Knowing the Names"; Jeffers, "Oh, Lovely Rock"

Comments:

5. **The Meaning of *Rich***

Authors: Philoxenes; Henry David Thoreau

Key ideas: definitions of rich and poor

Rhetorical methods: definition, comparison/contrast, analysis

See also: Merton, "Rain and the Rhinoceros"; Gregory, "Shame"; Jewett, "A White Heron"; Leopold, "Good Oak"; Berry, "Home of the Free"; Schumacher, "Buddhist Economics"

Comments:

6. **On Journeys**

Author: Calvin Rutstrom

Key ideas: the journey versus the destination; speed; goals

Rhetorical methods: example, comparison/contrast, cause/effect, argument, process, analysis

See also: Holm, "Horizontal Grandeur"; Kerwin, "The Anatomy of Ignorance"; Gould, "Darwin's Middle Road"; Holm, "The Grand Tour"; Didion, "On Keeping a Notebook"; Momaday, "The Way to Rainy Mountain"; Abbey, "Industrial Tourism"

Comments:

7. **On Leadership**

Author: Lao-Tzu, *Tao Te Ching* 17

    3 translations: Tolbert McCarroll; Stephen Mitchell; Gia-fu Feng and Jane English

Key ideas: leadership

Rhetorical methods: comparison/contrast, cause/effect, process, definition

See also: Hoff, "The Crooked Tree"; Beston, "Birds"; Shelley, "Ozymandias"; Leopold, "Good Oak"; Griffin, "I Like to Think of Harriet Tubman"; Morowitz, "Women's Lib and the Battle Against Entropy"

Comments:

8. **Foreseeing and Forestalling**

Author: Albert Schweitzer

Key ideas: foresee and forestall; anticipation and prevention of problems

Rhetorical methods: definition, example, process, cause/effect

See also: Gordon and Suzuki, "How Did We Come to This?"; Leopold, "Good Oak"; Lopez, "The Passing Wisdom of Birds"

Comments:

9. On Judging Quality

Author: Aldo Leopold

Key ideas: the process of perceiving quality; the meaning of "quality"

Rhetorical methods: example, narration, process

See also: Ehrlich, "About Men"; Hoff, "The Crooked Tree"; Holm, "Horizontal Grandeur"; Twain, "Two Ways of Seeing the River"; Thomas, " Scabies, Scrapie"

Comments:

10. Are We "Tools of Our Tools"?

Authors: Aldo Leopold; Henry David Thoreau

Key ideas: the connection between thought and action; effects of money

Rhetorical methods: process, cause/effect, narration, example, definition, analysis

See also: Berry, "Agricultural Solutions for Agricultural Problems"; Griffin, "Use"; Merton, "Rain and the Rhinoceros"; Abbey, "Industrial Tourism"; Schumacher, "Buddhist Economics"

Comments:

11. On Specialization

Author: Wendell Berry

Key ideas: helplessness and anxiety; experts and specialists

Rhetorical methods: description, cause/effect, argument, example, definition, classification, analysis

See also: Berry, "Home of the Free"; Kerwin, "The Anatomy of Ignorance"; Thomas, "Humanities and Science"; Berry, "Agricultural Solutions for Agricultural Problems"; Griffin, "Use"; Merton, "Rain and the Rhinoceros"; Twain, "Two Ways of Seeing the River"; Abbey, "Industrial Tourism"; Schumacher, "Buddhist Economics"

Comments:

Part Two: Reference Charts   43

12.   "See No Evil": Facing Facts

Author: Aldo Leopold

Key ideas: teaching of "real" facts; recognizing and facing unpleasant issues

Rhetorical methods: example, narration, cause/effect, process

See also: Deloria, "We Talk, You Listen"; Morowitz, "Women's Lib and the Battle Against Entropy"; Kerwin, "The Anatomy of Ignorance"; Thomas, "Humanities and Science"; Berry, "Agricultural Solutions for Agricultural Problems"; Griffin, "Use"; Gregory, "Shame"; Merton, "Rain and the Rhinoceros"; Kingston, "No Name Woman"; Carver, "My Father's Life"; Eiseley, "The Sparrow Hawk"; Lopez, "The Passing Wisdom of Birds"; Leopold, "Good Oak"; Gordon and Suzuki, "How Did We Come to This?"; Gore, "Ships in the Desert"; Williams, "The Clan of One-Breasted Women"; Griffin, "I Like to Think of Harriet Tubman"

Comments:

13.   What Do We Owe Future Generations?

Author: Great Law of the Haudenosaunee

Key ideas: impacts of decisions and laws into seven generations

Rhetorical methods: cause/effect, definition, argument, comparison/contrast

See also: Williams, "The Clan of One-Breasted Women"; Griffin, "Use"; Ferris, "The Persistence of Mystery"; Carson, "The Sense of Wonder"; Walker, "In Search of Our Mothers' Gardens"; Kingston, "No Name Woman"; Silko, "Lullaby"; Jeffers, "Oh, Lovely Rock"; Shelley, "Ozymandias"; Lopez, "The Passing Wisdom of Birds"; Momaday, "The Way to Rainy Mountain"; Leopold, "Good Oak"; Gordon and Suzuki, "How Did We Come to This?"; Gore, "Ships in the Desert"; Abbey, "Industrial Tourism"

Comments:

14.   The Value of Mistakes

Author: Aldo Leopold

Key ideas: effect of mistakes; limits; freedom to make mistakes in order to learn

Rhetorical methods: definition, argument, cause/effect, narration

See also: Abbey, "Industrial Tourism"; Abbey, "The Canyon"; Kerwin, "The Anatomy of Ignorance"; Gould, "Darwin's Middle Road"; Frost, "Fire and Ice"; Ozick, "The Seam of the Snail"; Berry, "The Grandmother"; Kingston, "No Name Woman"; Silko, "Lullaby"; Carver, "My Father's Life"; Frost, "The Death of the Hired Man"; Eiseley, "The Sparrow Hawk"; Lopez, "The Passing Wisdom of Birds"; Leopold, "Good Oak"; Gordon and Suzuki, "How Did We Come to This?"; Gore, "Ships in the Desert"; Williams, "The Clan of One-Breasted Women"; Morowitz, "Women's Lib and the Battle Against Entropy"

Comments:

15.   On the "Mental Eye"

Author: Aldo Leopold

Key ideas: perception; the quality of the mental eye; recreation

Rhetorical methods: definition, analysis

See also: Carson, "The Sense of Wonder"; Jeffers, "Oh, Lovely Rock"; Jewett, "A White Heron"; Kerwin, "The Anatomy of Ignorance"; Beston, "Birds"; Eiseley, "The Hidden Teacher"; Hoff, "The Crooked Tree"; Holm, "The Grand Tour"; Abbey, "The Canyon"; Merton, "Rain and the Rhinoceros"; Dickinson, "To Make a Prairie"; Holm, "Horizontal Grandeur"; Thoreau, "The Forest"; Dillard, "Seeing"; Abbey, "Industrial Tourism"; Ballata, "The Mental Eye"

Comments:

16.   Engaging Contraries

Author: Aldo Leopold

Key ideas: harmony with land; the land as an organism

Rhetorical methods: description, comparison/contrast, cause/effect, analysis

See also: Merton, "Rain and the Rhinoceros"; Silko, "Lullaby"; Beston, "Birds"; Berry, "Agricultural Solutions"; Griffin, "Use"; Holm, "Horizontal Grandeur"; Leopold, "Good Oak"; Gordon and Suzuki, "How Did We Come to This?"; Gore, "Ships in the Desert"; Williams, "The Clan of One-Breasted Women"; Schumacher, "Buddhist Economics"

Comments:

17. Making Things Come Alive

Author: Arthur Zajonc

Key ideas: relationship between knowing, seeing, and interpreting; perception; literacy

Rhetorical methods: narration, cause/effect, definition, analysis

See also: Dillard, "Seeing"; Thoreau, "The Forest"; Kerwin, "The Anatomy of Ignorance"; Carson, "The Sense of Wonder"; Beston, "Birds"; Mueller, "What the Dog Perhaps Hears"; Eiseley, "The Hidden Teacher"; Holm, "The Grand Tour"; Dickinson, "To Make a Prairie"; Holm, "Horizontal Grandeur"; Rupp, "Knowing the Names"; Twain, "Two Ways of Seeing the River"; Jeffers, "Oh, Lovely Rock"; Momaday, "The Way to Rainy Mountain"

Comments:

18. Standing Up for—What?

Author: Martin Niemoller

Key ideas: Nazi effect; speaking up

Rhetorical methods: definition, process, narration, example, argument

See also: Frost, "The Death of the Hired Man"; Walker, "In Search of Our Mothers' Gardens"; Williams, "The Clan of One-Breasted Women"; Holm, "The Grand Tour"; Gregory, "Shame"; Malcolm X, "How I Discovered Words"; Merton, "Rain and the Rhinoceros"; Silko, "Lullaby"; Eiseley, "The Sparrow Hawk"; Lopez, "The Passing Wisdom of Birds"; Jewett, "A White Heron"; Griffin, "I Like to Think of Harriet Tubman"; Morowitz, "Women's Lib and the Battle Against Entropy"; Abbey, "Industrial Tourism"; Deloria, "We Talk, You Listen"; Schumacher, "Buddhist Economics"

Comments:

19. Truth?

Authors: Blaise Pascal; John Fowles

Key ideas: understanding vs. existing; seeing the whole tree/truth; limitations of senses

Rhetorical methods: comparison/contrast, analysis, definition, example, narration, argument

Part Two: Reference Charts

See also: Raymo, "The Silence"; Mueller, "What the Dog Perhaps Hears"; Beston, "Birds"; Kerwin, "The Anatomy of Ignorance"; Ferris, "The Persistence of Mystery"; Eiseley, "The Hidden Teacher"; Holm, "The Grand Tour"; Hughes, "Theme for English B"; Merton, "Rain and the Rhinoceros"; Ozick, "The Seam of the Snail"; Didion, "On Keeping a Notebook"; Berry, "The Grandmother"; Walker, "In Search of Our Mothers' Gardens"; Kingston, "No Name Woman"; Silko, "Lullaby"; Ehrlich, "About Men"; Holm, "Horizontal Grandeur"; Thoreau, "The Forest"; Dillard, "Seeing"; Leopold, "The Deer Swath"; Rupp, "Knowing the Names"; Twain, "Two Ways of Seeing the River"; Eiseley, "The Sparrow Hawk"; Williams, "The Clan of One-Breasted Women"

Comments:

20. On Respect

Author: Standing Bear

Key ideas: respect; lack of respect; ownership

Rhetorical methods: process, definition, cause/effect, classification, argument

See also: Griffin, "Use"; Griffin, "I Like to Think of Harriet Tubman"; Thomas, "Humanities and Science"; Carson, "The Sense of Wonder"; Gregory, "Shame"; Walker, "In Search of Our Mothers' Gardens"; Silko, "Lullaby"; Ehrlich, "About Men"; Momaday, "The Way to Rainy Mountain"; Berry, "Home of the Free"; Schumacher, "Buddhist Economics"

Comments:

21. On Seeing

Author: Joseph Wood Krutch

Key idea: looking and seeing; awareness

Rhetorical methods: description, analysis

See also: Dillard, "Seeing"; Leopold, "The Deer Swath"; Didion, "On Keeping a Notebook"; Carson, "The Sense of Wonder"; Beston, "Birds"; Eiseley, "The Hidden Teacher"; Holm, "The Grand Tour"; Hughes, "Theme for English B"; Thoreau, "The Forest"; Rupp, "Knowing the Names"; Twain, "Two Ways of Seeing the River";

Jeffers, "Oh, Lovely Rock"; Momaday, "The Way to Rainy Mountain"; Jewett, "A White Heron"; Leopold, "Good Oak"; Morowitz, "Women's Lib and the Battle Against Entropy"; Berry, "Home of the Free"

Comments:

22. Can the Worthwhile Be Made Trivial?

Author: Aldo Leopold

Key ideas: what is too easy or too hard; becoming trivial

Rhetorical methods: classification, cause/effect, process, comparison/contrast, narration

See also: Ozick, "The Seam of the Snail"; Malcolm X, "How I Discovered Words"; Thomas, "Humanities and Science"; Hoff, "The Crooked Tree"; Lopez, "Icebergs and Cathedrals"; Momaday, "The Way to Rainy Mountain"; Jewett, "A White Heron"; Berry, "Home of the Free"; Abbey, "Industrial Tourism"; Schumacher, "Buddhist Economics"

Comments:

23. What Is Required for a Change in Ethics?

Author: Aldo Leopold

Key ideas: change in ethics; "intellectual emphasis, loyalties, affections, and convictions"

Rhetorical methods: process, cause/effect, narration, analysis

See also: Kerwin, "The Anatomy of Ignorance"; Ferris, "The Persistence of Mystery"; Carson, "The Sense of Wonder"; Beston, "Birds"; Holm, "The Grand Tour"; Berry, "Agricultural Solutions for Agricultural Problems"; Griffin, "Use"; Hughes, "Theme for English B"; Gregory, "Shame"; Merton, "Rain and the Rhinoceros"; Carver, "My Father's Life"; Eiseley, "The Sparrow Hawk"; Lopez, "The Passing Wisdom of Birds"; Jewett, "A White Heron"; Leopold, "Good Oak"; Gordon and Suzuki, "How Did We Come to This?"; Gore, "Ships in the Desert"; Williams, "The Clan of One-Breasted Women"; Griffin, "I Like to Think of Harriet Tubman"

Comments:

48   Part Two: Reference Charts

24.   On Affluence
Author: Wendell Berry
Key ideas: affluence; civilization; enough; extravagance
Rhetorical methods: definition, comparison/contrast, classification
See also: Schumacher, "Buddhist Economics"; Berry, "Home of the Free"; Holm, "The Grand Tour"; Berry, "Agricultural Solutions for Agricultural Problems"; Merton, "Rain and the Rhinoceros"; Lopez, "The Passing Wisdom of Birds"; Momaday, "The Way to Rainy Mountain"
Comments:

25.   On Literacy
Author: E. D. Hirsch
Key ideas: literacy; reading and writing
Rhetorical methods: example, description, narration, process, cause/effect, comparison/contrast, argument, definition, classification
See also: Malcolm X, "How I Discovered Words"; Rupp, "Knowing the Names"; Thomas, "Humanities and Science"; Hughes, "Theme for English B"; Gregory, "Shame"; Walker, "In Search of Our Mothers' Gardens"; Silko, "Lullaby"; Carver, "My Father's Life"; Frost, "The Death of the Hired Man"; Thomas, "Scabies, Scrapie"; Deloria, "We Talk, You Listen"
Comments:

26.   What Is Too Much of a Good Thing?
Author: Aldo Leopold
Key ideas: "safety, prosperity, comfort, long life, and dullness"
Rhetorical methods: comparison/contrast, cause/effect, argument
See also: Berry, "Home of the Free"; Lopez, "Icebergs and Cathedrals"; Kerwin, "The Anatomy of Ignorance"; Ferris, "The Persistence of Mystery"; Carson, "The Sense of Wonder"; Abbey, "The Canyon"; Merton, "Rain and the Rhinoceros"; Ozick, "The Seam of the Snail"; Didion, "On Keeping a Notebook"; Jewett, "A White Heron"; Griffin, "I Like to Think of Harriet Tubman"; Abbey, "Industrial Tourism"
Comments:

Part Two: Reference Charts   49

27.   Planting Barley, Harvesting Wheat

Author: Rumi

Key idea: "What you do comes back in the same form"

Rhetorical methods: example, narration, cause/effect

See also: Gregory, "Shame"; Lopez, "The Passing Wisdom of Birds"; Hoff, "The Crooked Tree"; Griffin, "Use"; Dillard, "Seeing"; Leopold, "The Deer Swath"; Eiseley, "The Sparrow Hawk"; Shelley, "Ozymandias"; Lopez, "The Passing Wisdom of Birds"; Gordon and Suzuki, "How Did We Come to This?"; Gore, "Ships in the Desert"; Thomas, "Scabies, Scrapie"; Berry, "Home of the Free"

Comments:

28.   On Order

Author: Confucius

Key ideas: government; personal discipline

Rhetorical methods: process, cause/effect, narration

See also: Carson, "The Sense of Wonder"; Shelley, "Ozymandias"; Hoff, "The Crooked Tree"; Lopez, "The Passing Wisdom of Birds"; Griffin, "I Like to Think of Harriet Tubman"; Schumacher, "Buddhist Economics"

Comments:

29.   The Value of Limits

Author: Christopher Vecsey

Key ideas: ethics; limitations of freedom; morally proper action

Rhetorical methods: comparison/contrast, narration, definition, cause/effect, process, argument

See also: Berry, "Home of the Free"; Abbey, "Industrial Tourism"; Holm, "The Grand Tour"; Griffin, "Use"; Kingston, "No Name Woman"; Silko, "Lullaby"; Frost, "The Death of the Hired Man"; Gordon and Suzuki, "How Did We Come to This?"; Gore, "Ships in the Desert"; Williams, "The Clan of One-Breasted Women"; Griffin, "I Like to Think of Harriet Tubman"; Morowitz, "Women's Lib and the Battle Against Entropy"; Deloria, "We Talk, You Listen"; Schumacher, "Buddhist Economics"

Comments:

30.   On Day and Night
Author: Henry Beston
Key ideas: night and day
Rhetorical methods: description, narration, comparison/contrast
See also: Beston, "Birds"; Jeffers, "Oh, Lovely Rock"; Raymo, "The Silence"; Holm, "The Grand Tour"; Lopez, "Icebergs and Cathedrals"; Merton, "Rain and the Rhinoceros"
Comments:

31.   Color
Author: Toni Morrison
Key ideas: dark, night, black
Rhetorical methods: description, comparison/contrast
See also: Carson, "The Sense of Wonder"; Holm, "Horizontal Grandeur"; Thoreau, "The Forest"; Dillard, "Seeing"
Comments:

32.   Friendship
Author: Aristotle
Key ideas: friendship
Rhetorical methods: example, definition, cause/effect
See also: Frost, "The Death of the Hired Man"; Thomas, "Scabies, Scrapie"; Silko, "Lullaby"; Morowitz, "Women's Lib and the Battle Against Entropy"; Berry, "Home of the Free"; Deloria, "We Talk, You Listen"
Comments:

33.   Preventing Problems in the First Place
Authors: E. F. Schumacher; Thomas Merton
Key ideas: solving vs. avoiding problems; causing problems then trying to solve them
Rhetorical methods: narration, process

See also: Schumacher, "Buddhist Economics"; Merton, "Rain and the Rhinoceros"; Berry, "Agricultural Solutions for Agricultural Problems"; Griffin, "Use"; Abbey, "The Canyon"; Leopold, "Good Oak"; Gordon and Suzuki, "How Did We Come to This?"; Gore, "Ships in the Desert"; Williams, "The Clan of One-Breasted Women"

Comments:

34.   On Caring

Author: David Orr (Elie Weisel)

Key ideas: Nazism, education, ethics

Rhetorical methods: example, narration, comparison/contrast, process

See also: Walker, "In Search of Our Mothers' Gardens"; Williams, "The Clan of One-Breasted Women"; Thomas, "Humanities and Science"; Carson, "The Sense of Wonder"; Eiseley, "The Hidden Teacher"; Hoff, "The Crooked Tree"; Berry, "Agricultural Solutions for Agricultural Problems"; Griffin, "Use"; Lopez, "Icebergs and Cathedrals"; Hughes, "Theme for English B"; Merton, "Rain and the Rhinoceros"; Lopez, "The Passing Wisdom of Birds"; Momaday, "The Way to Rainy Mountain"; Berry, "Home of the Free"

Comments:

35.   On Awareness

Authors: Norman Maclean; Henry David Thoreau

Key ideas: thinking and seeing

Rhetorical methods: process, narration, cause/effect

See also: Thoreau, "The Forest"; Dillard, "Seeing"; Carson, "The Sense of Wonder"; Beston, "Birds"; Raymo, "The Silence"; Hoff, "The Crooked Tree"; Holm, "The Grand Tour"; Holm, "Horizontal Grandeur"; Leopold, "The Deer Swath"

Comments:

36.   Seeing "Near and Narrowly"

Author: Henry David Thoreau

Key ideas: seeing; intention; looking far and wide or near and narrow

Rhetorical methods: description, comparison/contrast

See also: Thoreau, "The Forest"; Holm, "Horizontal Grandeur"; Thomas, "Humanities and Science"; Gould, "Darwin's Middle Road"; Carson, "The Sense of Wonder"; Beston, "Birds"; Hughes, "Theme for English B"; Gregory, "Shame"; Ozick, "The Seam of the Snail"; Berry, "The Grandmother"; Walker, "In Search of Our Mothers' Gardens"; Kingston, "No Name Woman"; Silko, "Lullaby"; Ehrlich, "About Men"; Carver, "My Father's Life"; Frost, "The Death of the Hired Man"; Shelley, "Ozymandias"; Momaday, "The Way to Rainy Mountain"; Williams, "The Clan of One-Breasted Women"; Deloria, "We Talk, You Listen"

Comments:

37.   Looking versus Seeing

Authors: Rachel Carson; Oscar Wilde

Key idea: seeing

Rhetorical method: description

See also: Carson, "The Sense of Wonder"; Holm, "The Grand Tour"; Mowat, "Naked to the Wolves"; Beston, "Birds"; Raymo, "The Silence"; Eiseley, "The Hidden Teacher"; Hoff, "The Crooked Tree"; Didion, "On Keeping a Notebook"; Berry, "The Grandmother"; Silko, "Lullaby"; Ehrlich, "About Men"; Holm, "Horizontal Grandeur"; Thoreau, "The Forest"; Dillard, "Seeing"; Leopold, "The Deer Swath"; Rupp, "Knowing the Names"; Twain, "Two Ways of Seeing the River"; Eiseley, The Sparrow Hawk"; Jeffers, "Oh, Lovely Rock"; Jewett, "A White Heron"; Deloria, "We Talk, You Listen"

Comments:

38.   What Is a Good Education?

Author: Wendell Berry

Key ideas: education; writer vs. man

Rhetorical method: definition

See also: Kerwin, "The Anatomy of Ignorance"; Thomas, "Humanities and Science"; Eiseley, "The Hidden Teacher"; Hoff, "The Crooked Tree"; Hughes, "Theme for English B"; Gregory, "Shame"; Malcolm X, "How I Discovered Words"; Thomas, "Scabies, Scrapie"

Comments:

39.   The Experience of Art and the Art of Experience
Author: John Fowles
Key ideas: art vs. technique; creativity
Rhetorical method: comparison/contrast
See also: Walker, "In Search of Our Mothers' Gardens"; Gould, "Darwin's Middle Way"; Lopez, "Icebergs and Cathedrals"; Ozick, "The Seam of the Snail"; Frost, "The Death of the Hired Man"

Comments:

40.   The Importance of Ignorance
Authors: Ann Kerwin; Lewis Thomas; Karl Popper
Key idea: ignorance
Rhetorical methods: example, classification, analysis
See also: Kerwin, "The Anatomy of Ignorance"; Thomas, "Humanities and Science"; Ferris, "The Persistence of Mystery"; Gould, "Darwin's Middle Road"; Carson "The Sense of Wonder"; Beston, "Birds"; Raymo, "The Silence"; Mueller, "What the Dog Perhaps Hears"; Eiseley, "The Hidden Teacher"; Gordon and Suzuki, "How Did We Come to This?"; Gore, "Ships in the Desert"; Williams, "The Clan of One-Breasted Women"; Thomas, "Scabies, Scrapie"; Deloria, "We Talk, You Listen"

Comments:

41.   On Thinking
Author: Hannah Arendt
Key ideas: thinking; solitude; conscience; right and wrong
Rhetorical methods: narration, cause/effect

54   Part Two: Reference Charts

See also: Merton, "Rain and the Rhinoceros"; Jewett, "A White Heron"; Holm, "The Grand Tour"; Frost, "The Death of the Hired Man"; Eiseley, "The Sparrow Hawk"; Lopez, "The Passing Wisdom of Birds"; Morowitz, "Women's Lib and the Battle Against Entropy"; Berry, "Home of the Free"; Schumacher, "Buddhist Economics"; Ballata, "The Mental Eye"

Comments:

42.   On Learning to Love Life

Authors: James Baldwin; Erich Fromm

Key ideas: children; imitation; learning; love of life v. love of death

Rhetorical methods: process, example, comparison/contrast, cause/effect, analysis

See also: Carson, "The Sense of Wonder"; Griffin, "Use"; Hughes, "Theme for English B"; Gregory, "Shame"; Malcolm X, "How I Discovered Words"; Ozick, "The Seam of the Snail"; Didion, "On Keeping a Notebook"; Walker, "In Search of Our Mothers' Gardens"; Silko, "Lullaby"; Carver, "My Father's Life"; Momaday, "The Way to Rainy Mountain"; Jewett, "A White Heron"

Comments:

43.   Time

Author: Ben Hutchcraft

Key ideas: Bennett Juniper; age; perspective

Rhetorical methods: process, narration

See also: Berry, "The Grandmother"; Walker, "In Search of Our Mothers' Gardens"; Kingston, "No Name Woman"; Silko, "Lullaby"; Ehrlich, "About Men"; Carver, "My Father's Life"; Frost, "The Death of the Hired Man"; Momaday, "The Way to Rainy Mountain"; Jewett, "A White Heron"; Williams, "The Clan of One-Breasted Women"; Griffin, "I Like to Think of Harriet Tubman"

Comments:

44. Conquering

Author: Aldo Leopold

Key idea: the conqueror role and attitude

Rhetorical methods: description, cause/effect

See also: Kerwin, "The Anatomy of Ignorance"; Griffin, "Use"; Lopez, "The Passing Wisdom of Birds"; Ferris, "The Persistence of Mystery"; Beston, "Birds"; Holm, "The Grand Tour"; Berry, "Agricultural Solutions for Agricultural Problems"; Hughes, "Theme for English B"; Merton, "Rain and the Rhinoceros"; Walker, "In Search of Our Mothers' Gardens"; Eiseley, "The Sparrow Hawk"; Shelley, "Ozymandias"; Leopold, "Good Oak"; Gordon and Suzuki, "How Did We Come to This?"; Gore, "Ships in the Desert"; Williams, "The Clan of One-Breasted Women"; Griffin, "I Like to Think of Harriet Tubman"; Deloria, "We Talk, You Listen"

Comments:

45. On Excellence

Author: Edward Abbey

Key idea: excellence and value, difficult and rare

Rhetorical methods: cause/effect, definition, comparison/contrast, process

See also: Abbey, "Industrial Tourism"; Hoff, "The Crooked Tree"; Gould, "Darwin's Middle Road"; Ozick, "The Seam of the Snail"

Comments:

46. Aiming

Author: Henry David Thoreau

Key ideas: aim; goals

Rhetorical methods: example, comparison/contrast, narration, cause/effect, argument, analysis

See also: Malcolm X, "How I Discovered Words"; Gordon and Suzuki, "How Did We Come to This?"; Thomas, "Humanities and Science"; Eiseley, "The Hidden Teacher"; Lopez, "Icebergs and Cathedrals"; Berry, "The Grandmother"; Walker, "In Search of Our Mothers' Gardens"; Shelley, "Ozymandias"; Lopez, "The Passing Wisdom of Birds"; Griffin, "I Like to Think of Harriet Tubman"; Schumacher, "Buddhist Economics"; Ballata, "The Mental Eye"

Comments:

47. The Centrifugal and the Centripetal in Writing
Author: Phyllis Ballata
Key ideas: pulling out ideas; pulling in or condensing ideas
Rhetorical methods: comparison/contrast, writing process
See also: Ballata, "The Mental Eye"
Comments:

48. What Does Television Provide?
Author: Guy Lyon Playfair
Key idea: problems of television
Rhetorical method: argument
See also: Carson, "The Sense of Wonder"; Eiseley, "The Hidden Teacher"; Malcolm X, "How I Discovered Words"; Merton, "Rain and the Rhinoceros"; Leopold, "The Deer Swath"; Abbey, "Industrial Tourism"; Deloria, "We Talk, You Listen"
Comments:

49. What Is "Right"?
Author: Aldo Leopold
Key ideas: right and wrong; Leopold's Maxim
Rhetorical methods: definition, comparison/contrast, analysis, argument
See also: Griffin, "Use"; Jewett, "A White Heron"; Thomas, "Humanities and Science"; Berry, "Agricultural Solutions for Agricultural Problems"; Merton, "Rain and the Rhinoceros"; Dickinson, "To Make a Prairie"; Holm, "Horizontal Grandeur"; Eiseley, "The Sparrow Hawk"; Lopez, "The Passing Wisdom of Birds"; Leopold, "Good Oak"; Gordon and Suzuki, "How Did We Come to This?"; Gore, "Ships in the Desert"; Williams, "The Clan of One-Breasted Women"; Berry, "Home of the Free"; Abbey, "Industrial Tourism"; Schumacher, "Buddhist Economics"
Comments:

50. Irony

Author: Edward Abbey

Key ideas: sportsmanship and animals; irony

Rhetorical methods: argument, description, definition

See also: Abbey, "Industrial Tourism"; Deloria, "We Talk, You Listen"; Shelley, "Ozymandias"

Comments:

51. Fact versus Interpretation

Authors: Charles Marion Russell; Edward Abbey

Key ideas: "A pioneer destroys things and calls it civilization"; "Growth for the sake of growth is cancerous madness"; what is fact and what is interpretation?

Rhetorical methods: analysis, comparison/contrast, argument

See also: Abbey, "Industrial Tourism"; Schumacher, "Buddhist Economics"; Mueller, "What a Dog Perhaps Hears"; Eiseley, "The Hidden Teacher"; Hoff, "The Crooked Tree"; Holm, "The Grand Tour"; Griffin, "Use"; Kingston, "No Name Woman"; Silko, "Lullaby"; Carver, "My Father's Life"; Frost, "The Death of the Hired Man"; Dillard, "Seeing"; Leopold, "The Deer Swath"; Twain, "Two Ways of Seeing the River"; Leopold, "Good Oak"; Gordon and Suzuki, "How Did We Come to This?"; Gore, "Ships in the Desert"; Williams, "The Clan of One-Breasted Women"; Berry, "Home of the Free"

Comments:

52. Seeing What Is There Instead of What We Expect

Author: Wendell Berry

Key ideas: "see and respect what is there"; vision versus sight

Rhetorical methods: description, cause/effect, definition, example, process

See also: Holm, "Horizontal Grandeur"; Deloria, "We Talk, You Listen"; Beston, "Birds"; Hoff, "The Crooked Tree"; Holm, "The Grand Tour"; Berry, "Agricultural Solutions for Agricultural Problems"; Griffin, "Use"; Hughes, "Theme for English B"; Gregory, "Shame"; Mowat, "Naked to the Wolves"; Ozick, "The Seam of the Snail"; Walker, "In Search of Our Mothers' Gardens"; Silko, "Lullaby";

58   Part Two: Reference Charts

Ehrlich, "About Men"; Frost, "The Death of the Hired Man"; Jeffers, "Oh, Lovely Rock"; Lopez, "The Passing Wisdom of Birds"; Momaday, "The Way to Rainy Mountain"; Gordon and Suzuki, "How Did We Come to This?"; Gore, "Ships in the Desert"; Williams, "The Clan of One-Breasted Women"; Abbey, "Industrial Tourism"; Schumacher, "Buddhist Economics"

Comments:

53.   What's in a Word?

Authors: Bible, Philippians 4:8; Frederick Jackson Turner

Key ideas: thought and action

Rhetorical methods: definition, cause/effect, comparison/contrast

See also: Griffin, "I Like to Think of Harriet Tubman"; Berry, "Home of the Free"; Schumacher, "Buddhist Economics"; Kerwin, "The Anatomy of Ignorance"; Thomas, "Humanities and Science"; Carson, "The Sense of Wonder"; Hoff, "The Crooked Tree"; Berry, "Agricultural Solutions for Agricultural Problems"; Griffin, "Use"; Leopold, "The Deer Swath"; Rupp, "Knowing the Names"; Gordon and Suzuki, "How Did We Come to This?"; Gore, "Ships in the Desert"; Williams, "The Clan of One-Breasted Women"; Griffin, "I Like to Think of Harriet Tubman"; Berry, "Home of the Free"

Comments:

54.   Making What's Difficult Look Easy

Author: Pablo Casals

Key ideas: "Art is the product of labor"; paying your dues

Rhetorical methods: narration, process, comparison/contrast, cause/effect

See also: Didion, "On Keeping a Notebook"; Ozick, "The Seam of the Snail"; Gould, "Darwin's Middle Road"; Lopez, "Icebergs and Cathedrals"

Comments:

55.   On Reading

Authors: Francis Bacon; Erich Fromm; Gilbert Highet

Key ideas: books as minds and hearts speaking; reading as conversation

Rhetorical methods: description, comparison/contrast

Part Two: Reference Charts   59

See also: Malcolm X, "How I Discovered Words"; Hughes, "Theme for English B"; Mueller, "What the Dog Perhaps Hears"; Holm, "The Grand Tour"; Griffin, "Use"; Abbey, "The Canyon"; Berry, "The Grandmother"; Jeffers, "Oh, Lovely Rock"; Lopez, "The Passing Wisdom of Birds"; Momaday, "The Way to Rainy Mountain"; Williams, "The Clan of One-Breasted Women"; Griffin, "I Like to Think of Harriet Tubman"

Comments:

56.   On Finding the Essence
Author: D. H. Lawrence
Key idea: creativity and art
Rhetorical methods: description, writing process
See also: Mueller, "What the Dog Perhaps Hears"; Hoff, "The Crooked Tree"; Frost, "Fire and Ice"; Hughes, "Theme for English B"; Berry, "The Grandmother"; Dickinson, "To Make a Prairie"; Shelley, "Ozymandias"

Comments:

57.   The Aims of Advertising
Author: Christopher Lasch
Key idea: advertising
Rhetorical methods: description, classification, cause/effect, comparison/contrast
See also: Merton, "Rain and the Rhinoceros"; Gordon and Suzuki, "How Did We Come to This?"; Gore, "Ships in the Desert"; Berry, "Home of the Free"; Abbey, "Industrial Tourism"; Deloria, "We Talk, You Listen"; Schumacher, "Buddhist Economics"

Comments:

58.   On Doing Work You Love
Author: Rumi
Key idea: "Let the beauty we love be what we do."
Rhetorical methods: process, cause/effect

See also: Kerwin, "The Anatomy of Ignorance"; Thomas, "Humanities and Science"; Hoff, "The Crooked Tree"; Ozick, "The Seam of the Snail"; Walker, "In Search of Our Mothers' Gardens"; Ehrlich, "About Men"; Jewett, "A White Heron"; Schumacher, "Buddhist Economics"

Comments:

59.   Preparing for Good Luck

Authors: Ernest Hemingway; Louis Pasteur

Key ideas: skill versus luck; the prepared mind

Rhetorical methods: cause/effect, process

See also: Ferris, "The Persistence of Mystery"; Thoreau, "The Forest"; Kerwin, "The Anatomy of Ignorance"; Thomas, "Humanities and Science"; Gould, "Darwin's Middle Road"; Carson, "The Sense of Wonder"; Beston, "Birds"; Raymo, "The Silence"; Eiseley, "The Hidden Teacher"; Dillard, "Seeing"; Leopold, "The Deer Swath"; Rupp, "Knowing the Names"

Comments:

60.   Asking the Right Questions

Author: Sidney Harris; William Devall

Key ideas: questioning; control over the questions

Rhetorical methods: process, cause/effect

See also: Kerwin, "The Anatomy of Ignorance"; Mowat, "Naked to the Wolves"; Gordon and Suzuki, "How Did We Come to This?"; Williams, "The Clan of One-Breasted Women"; Griffin, "I Like to Think of Harriet Tubman"; Abbey, "Industrial Tourism"; Schumacher, "Buddhist Economics"; Berry, "Agricultural Solutions for Agricultural Problems"; Griffin, "Use"; Hughes, "Theme for English B"; Leopold, "Good Oak"; Gore, "Ships in the Desert"

Comments:

61.   Being Alone

Authors: Anne Morrow Lindbergh; Loren Eiseley; John Muir

Key ideas: loneliness; solitude; sympathy and relationship; separation

Rhetorical methods: example, cause/effect, analysis, definition, comparison/contrast, description, classification

Part Two: Reference Charts   61

See also: Merton, "Rain and the Rhinoceros"; Holm, "The Grand Tour"; Abbey, "The Canyon"; Silko, "Lullaby"; Ehrlich, "About Men"; Frost, "The Death of the Hired Man"; Dillard, "Seeing"; Leopold, "The Deer Swath"; Jeffers, "Oh, Lovely Rock"; Momaday, "The Way to Rainy Mountain"; Jewett, "A White Heron"; Williams, "The Clan of One-Breasted Women"; Abbey, "Industrial Tourism"

Comments:

62.   Knowing One's Self

Authors: Edna St. Vincent Millay; Lao-Tzu; St. Augustine; John Steinbeck; Joseph Wood Krutch

Key ideas: knowing one's self; wisdom and enlightenment; wonder; fear

Rhetorical methods: description, example, classification, analysis, argument, process

See also: Momaday, "The Way to Rainy Mountain"; Hughes, "Theme for English B"; Kerwin, "The Anatomy of Ignorance"; Ferris, "The Persistence of Mystery"; Carson, "The Sense of Wonder"; Eiseley, "The Hidden Teacher"; Hoff, "The Crooked Tree"; Frost, "Fire and Ice"; Abbey, "The Canyon"; Merton, "Rain and the Rhinoceros"; Ozick, "The Seam of the Snail"; Didion, "On Keeping a Notebook"; Lopez, "The Passing Wisdom of Birds"; Williams, "The Clan of One-Breasted Women"; Thomas, "Scabies, Scrapie"

Comments:

63.   Defining Freedom

Authors: Percy Bysshe Shelley; John Milton

Key ideas: freedom as individualism; freedom in community

Rhetorical method: definition

See also: Berry, "Home of the Free"; Griffin, "Use"; Abbey, "The Canyon"; Merton, "Rain and the Rhinoceros"; Shelley, "Ozymandias"; Momaday, "The Way to Rainy Mountain"; Leopold, "Good Oak"; Griffin, "I Like to Think of Harriet Tubman"; Morowitz, "Women's Lib and the Battle Against Entropy"; Schumacher, "Buddhist Economics"

Comments:

64. One for All or One for One

Author: Frederick Jackson Turner

Key ideas: conflicts in democratic ideals; individual versus community

Rhetorical methods: classification, process, example, comparison/contrast

See also: Silko, "Lullaby"; Williams, "The Clan of the One-Breasted Women"; Griffin, "I Like to Think of Harriet Tubman"; Merton, "Rain and the Rhinoceros"; Frost, "The Death of the Hired Man"; Momaday, "The Way to Rainy Mountain"; Leopold, "Good Oak"; Gordon and Suzuki, "How Did We Come to This?"; Gore, "Ships in the Desert"; Abbey, "Industrial Tourism"; Schumacher, "Buddhist Economics"

Comments:

65. Do Unto Others . . . ?

Author: Thomas Merton

Key idea: Natural Law (Golden Rule)

Rhetorical methods: cause/effect, comparison/contrast, argument

See also: Merton, "Rain and the Rhinoceros"; Berry, "Agricultural Solutions for Agricultural Problems"; Hoff, "The Crooked Tree"; Griffin, "Use"; Gregory, "Shame"; Walker, "In Search of Our Mothers' Gardens"; Silko, "Lullaby"; Carver, "My Father's Life"; Shelley, "Ozymandias"; Lopez, "The Passing Wisdom of Birds"; Griffin, "I Like to Think of Harriet Tubman"; Thomas, "Scabies, Scrapie"; Morowitz, "Women's Lib and the Battle Against Entropy"; Deloria, "We Talk, You Listen"; Schumacher, "Buddhist Economics"

Comments:

66. What Is Happiness?

Author: Thomas Merton

Key ideas: true happiness; good of others

Rhetorical methods: definition, description, comparison/contrast, cause/effect, argument

See also: Merton, "Rain and the Rhinoceros"; Thomas, "Scabies, Scrapie"; Carson, "The Sense of Wonder"; Hoff, "The Crooked Tree"; Griffin, "Use"; Gregory, "Shame"; Eiseley, "The Sparrow Hawk"; Jewett, "A White Heron"; Morowitz, "Women's Lib and the Battle Against Entropy"; Schumacher, "Buddhist Economics"

Comments:

67.   Means and Ends

Authors: Ortega y Gasset; E. F. Schumacher

Key ideas: ideas; living; choosing

Rhetorical methods: definition, process, argument, comparison/contrast

See also: Schumacher, "Buddhist Economics"; Kerwin, "The Anatomy of Ignorance"; Thomas, "Humanities and Science"; Holm, "The Grand Tour"; Berry, "Agricultural Solutions for Agricultural Problems"; Griffin, "Use"; Lopez, "Icebergs and Cathedrals"; Merton, "Rain and the Rhinoceros"; Lopez, "The Passing Wisdom of Birds"; Gordon and Suzuki, "How Did We Come to This?"; Ballata, "The Mental Eye"

Comments:

68.   Words and Ideas

Author: E. F. Schumacher

Key ideas: words; ideas; thinking

Rhetorical methods: cause/effect, description, example, argument, comparison/contrast

See also: Malcolm X, "How I Discovered Words"; Berry, "Agricultural Solutions for Agricultural Problems"; Schumacher, "Buddhist Economics"; Thomas, "Humanities and Science"; Griffin, "Use"; Merton, "Rain and the Rhinoceros"; Ozick, "The Seam of the Snail"; Didion, "On Keeping a Notebook"; Rupp, "Knowing the Names"; Morowitz, "Women's Lib and the Battle Against Entropy"

Comments:

69.   Enjoyments
Author: Charles Darwin
Key ideas: loss of art, music, and poetry as loss of happiness, intellect, and character
Rhetorical methods: comparison/contrast, process, argument, cause/effect
See also: Gould, "Darwin's Middle Road"; Carson, "The Sense of Wonder"; Thomas, "Scabies, Scrapie"; Thomas, "Humanities and Science"; Ferris, "The Persistence of Mystery"
Comments:

70.   What Should Work Be?
Author: E. F. Schumacher
Key idea: "soul-destroying, meaningless, mechanical, monotonous, moronic work"
Rhetorical methods: definition, cause/effect, description, analysis
See also: Schumacher, "Buddhist Economics"; Berry, "Home of the Free"; Lopez, "Icebergs and Cathedrals"; Berry, "Agricultural Solutions for Agricultural Problems"; Griffin, "Use"; Walker, "In Search of Our Mothers' Gardens"; Ehrlich, "About Men"; Carver, "My Father's Life"; Twain, "Two Ways of Seeing the River"; Eiseley, "The Sparrow Hawk"; Morowitz, "Women's Lib and the Battle Against Entropy"
Comments:

71.   On Recreation
Authors: Gilbert K. Chesterton; Aldo Leopold
Key ideas: the perceptive faculty; the mental eye
Rhetorical methods: narration, analysis, description
See also: Carson, "The Sense of Wonder"; Beston, "Birds"; Holm, "Horizontal Grandeur"; Holm, "The Grand Tour"; Kerwin, "The Anatomy of Ignorance"; Eiseley, "The Hidden Teacher"; Hoff, "The Crooked Tree"; Lopez, "Icebergs and Cathedrals"; Merton, "Rain and the Rhinoceros"; Thoreau, "The Forest"; Dillard, "Seeing"; Leopold, "The Deer Swath"; Rupp, "Knowing the Names"; Jeffers, "Oh, Lovely Rock"; Jewett, "A White Heron"; Abbey, "Industrial Tourism"
Comments:

Part Two: Reference Charts   65

72.   What Are Stories For?
Authors: Tim O'Brien; Toni Morrison; Leslie Marmon Silko
Key ideas: fact and truth; fiction; unique and universal; storytelling
Rhetorical methods: definition, comparison/contrast
See also: Silko, "Lullaby"; Kingston, "No Name Woman"; Momaday, "The Way to Rainy Mountain"; Jewett, "A White Heron"; Hoff, "The Crooked Tree"; Hughes, "Theme for English B"; Berry, "The Grandmother"; Frost, "The Death of the Hired Man"; Jeffers, "Oh, Lovely Rock"; Shelley, "Ozymandias"
Comments:

73.   Are You Raw or Cooked?
Author: Gary Snyder
Key ideas: raw person versus cooked person; respect and familiarity
Rhetorical methods: description, comparison/contrast
See also: Mueller, "What the Dog Perhaps Hears"; Hughes, "Theme for English B"; Berry, "The Grandmother"; Frost, "The Death of the Hired Man"; Hoff, "The Crooked Tree"; Merton, "Rain and the Rhinoceros"; Ozick, "The Seam of the Snail"; Walker, "In Search of Our Mothers' Gardens"; Carver, "My Father's Life"; Momaday, "The Way to Rainy Mountain"; Deloria, "We Talk, You Listen"
Comments:

74.   On Taking Time
Author: Sister Jose Hobday's Seneca Mother
Key idea: peace and happiness from taking time to do work completely
Rhetorical methods: argument, comparison/contrast, cause/effect, process, narrative
See also: Momaday, "The Way to Rainy Mountain"; Morowitz, "Women's Lib and the Battle Against Entropy"; Carson, "The Sense of Wonder"; Beston, "Birds"; Leopold, "Good Oak"; Berry, "Home of the Free"; Abbey, "Industrial Tourism"; Schumacher, "Buddhist Economics"
Comments:

75. "The Proper University Product"
Author: Wendell Berry
Key ideas: education; specialized expertise versus competence in all concerns
Rhetorical methods: definition, comparison/contrast
See also: Kerwin, "The Anatomy of Ignorance"; Thomas, "Humanities and Science"; Ferris, "The Persistence of Mystery"; Raymo, "The Silence"; Thomas, "Scabies, Scrapie"; Berry, "Home of the Free"
Comments:

76. On Spiritual Fruit
Author: Bible, Galatians 5:22–23
Key idea: the fruit of the Spirit
Rhetorical methods: definition, comparison/contrast
See also: Malcolm X, "How I Discovered Words"; Merton, "Rain and the Rhinoceros"
Comments:

77. Whose Shoulders Are You Standing On?
Authors: Bernard of Chartres; Sir Isaac Newton
Key idea: sitting on the shoulders of giants
Rhetorical methods: description, narration
See also: Momaday, "The Way to Rainy Mountain"; Deloria, "We Talk, You Listen"; Walker, "In Search of Our Mothers' Gardens"; Kingston, "No Name Woman"; Kerwin, "The Anatomy of Ignorance"; Ferris, "The Persistence of Mystery"; Carson, "The Sense of Wonder"; Lopez, "Icebergs and Cathedrals"; Ozick, "The Seam of the Snail"; Carver, "My Father's Life"; Williams, "The Clan of One-Breasted Women"; Griffin, "I Like to Think of Harriet Tubman"
Comments:

78. On Growing Old

Author: Maya Angelou

Key idea: "On Aging"

Rhetorical methods: definition, narration, example, process, cause/effect, comparison/contrast, classification

See also: Silko, "Lullaby"; Williams, "The Clan of One-Breasted Women"; Carver, "My Father's Life"; Frost, "The Death of the Hired Man"; Berry, "The Grandmother"; Momaday, "The Way to Rainy Mountain"

Comments:

79. Sin and Virtue

Key ideas: Seven Deadly Sins and Four Cardinal Virtues

Rhetorical methods: definition, cause/effect

See also:

Comments:

80. Is "Know-How" Enough?

Author: E. F. Schumacher

Key ideas: know-how; education; ideas of value; wisdom

Rhetorical methods: definition, description, process, example, classification, comparison/contrast, cause/effect, narration

See also: Kerwin, "The Anatomy of Ignorance"; Thomas, "Humanities and Science"; Ferris, "The Persistence of Mystery"; Carson, "The Sense of Wonder"; Eiseley, "The Hidden Teacher"; Hoff, "The Crooked Tree"; Berry, "Agricultural Solutions for Agricultural Problems"; Griffin, "Use"; Merton, "Rain and the Rhinoceros"; Lopez, "The Passing Wisdom of Birds"; Leopold, "Good Oak"; Gordon and Suzuki, "How Did We Come to This?"; Gore, "Ships in the Desert"; Williams, "The Clan of One-Breasted Women"; Berry, "Home of the Free"; Schumacher, "Buddhist Economics"; Ballata, "The Mental Eye"

Comments:

81.   On Leveling Down

Author: Henry David Thoreau

Key ideas: leveling down to the dullest; common sense; equality

Rhetorical methods: definition, description, cause/effect, argument

See also: Shelley, "Ozymandias"; Thomas, "Scabies, Scrapie"; Kerwin, "The Anatomy of Ignorance"; Thomas, "Humanities and Science"; Gould, "Darwin's Middle Road"; Lopez, "Icebergs and Cathedrals"; Hughes, "Theme for English B"; Malcolm X, "How I Discovered Words"; Merton, "Rain and the Rhinoceros"; Walker, "In Search of Our Mothers' Gardens"; Rupp, "Knowing the Names"; Griffin, "I Like to Think of Harriet Tubman"; Berry, "Home of the Free"; Abbey, "Industrial Tourism"

Comments:

82.   Keeping Your Thought

Author: Henry David Thoreau

Key ideas: keep your thought; freedom in the mind; brainwashing

Rhetorical methods: example, narration, process, cause/effect

See also: Malcolm X, "How I Discovered Words"; Deloria, "We Talk, You Listen"; Momaday, "The Way to Rainy Mountain"; Walker, "In Search of Our Mothers' Gardens"; Kerwin, "The Anatomy of Ignorance"; Carson, "The Sense of Wonder"; Hughes, "Theme for English B"; Jewett, "A White Heron"

Comments:

83.   A Question of Conscience: Legal versus Just

Author: Henry David Thoreau

Key ideas: law and right; conscience; justice (Martin Luther King, Jr., and Mohandas Gandhi)

Rhetorical methods: process, cause/effect, argument

See also: Kerwin, "The Anatomy of Ignorance"; Williams, "The Clan of One-Breasted Women"; Holm, "The Grand Tour"; Griffin, "Use"; Merton, "Rain and the Rhinoceros"; Walker, "In Search of Our Mothers' Gardens"; Silko, "Lullaby"; Eiseley, "The Sparrow

Hawk"; Lopez, "The Passing Wisdom of Birds"; Momaday, "The Way to Rainy Mountain"; Gordon and Suzuki, "How Did We Come to This?"; Gore, "Ships in the Desert"; Griffin, "I Like to Think of Harriet Tubman"; Deloria, "We Talk, You Listen"

Comments:

84.   On Appearance and Reality
Authors: Socrates; Hannah Arendt
Key ideas: "Be as you wish to appear"; appearance, choices, character
Rhetorical methods: argument, cause/effect
See also: Kerwin, "The Anatomy of Ignorance"; Hoff, "The Crooked Tree"; Hughes, "Theme for English B"; Malcolm X, "How I Discovered Words"; Ozick, "The Seam of the Snail"; Didion, "On Keeping a Notebook"; Walker, "In Search of Our Mothers' Gardens"; Ehrlich, "About Men"; Thomas, "Scabies, Scrapie"; Berry, "Home of the Free"; Deloria, "We Talk, You Listen"

Comments:

85.   Wasting the Body, Wasting the Spirit
Author: Wendell Berry
Key ideas: cultural wasting and weakening of body and spirit
Rhetorical method: argument
See also: Berry, "Home of the Free"; Carson, "The Sense of Wonder"; Holm, "The Grand Tour"; Griffin, "Use"; Lopez, "Icebergs and Cathedrals"; Merton, "Rain and the Rhinoceros"; Ozick, "The Seam of the Snail"; Didion, "On Keeping a Notebook"; Eiseley, "The Sparrow Hawk"; Lopez, "The Passing Wisdom of Birds"; Momaday, "The Way to Rainy Mountain"; Abbey, "Industrial Tourism"; Schumacher, "Buddhist Economics"

Comments:

86.   On Appetite and Anticipation
Author: Laurie Lee
Key ideas: appetite; anticipation
Rhetorical methods: cause/effect, definition, argument, process

Part Two: Reference Charts

See also: Kerwin, "The Anatomy of Ignorance"; Thomas, "Humanities and Science"; Ferris, "The Persistence of Mystery"; Carson, "The Sense of Wonder"; Griffin, "Use"; Malcolm X, "How I Discovered Words"; Merton, "Rain and the Rhinoceros"; Thoreau, "The Forest"; Dillard, "Seeing"; Leopold, "The Deer Swath"; Berry, "Home of the Free"; Schumacher, "Buddhist Economics"

Comments:

87.   Are You Fenced In?

Author: Loren Eiseley (See Darwin #69)

Key ideas: scientists and art and emotion; institutionalization of method; dogma

Rhetorical methods: comparison/contrast, cause/effect, argument, analysis

See also: Kerwin, "The Anatomy of Ignorance"; Thomas, "Humanities and Science"; Thomas, "Scabies, Scrapie"; Gould, "Darwin's Middle Road"; Ferris, "The Persistence of Mystery"; Carson, "The Sense of Wonder"; Beston, "Birds"; Eiseley, "The Hidden Teacher"; Lopez, "Icebergs and Cathedrals"; Gordon and Suzuki, "How Did We Come to This?"; Gore, "Ships in the Desert"; Abbey, "Industrial Tourism"; Schumacher, "Buddhist Economics"; Ballata, "The Mental Eye"

Comments:

88.   And Who Is My Neighbor?

Author: Wendell Berry

Key ideas: being a neighbor, workman, and salesman

Rhetorical methods: example, description, definition, process, argument

See also: Abbey, "Industrial Tourism"; Schumacher, "Buddhist Economics"; Gore, "Ships in the Desert"; Berry, "Agricultural Solutions for Agricultural Problems"; Gregory, "Shame"; Merton, "Rain and the Rhinoceros"; Carver, "My Father's Life"; Frost, "The Death of the Hired Man"; Leopold, "Good Oak"; Gordon and Suzuki, "How Did We Come to This?"; Williams, "The Clan of One-Breasted Women"; Berry, "Home of the Free"

Comments:

89. On Imagination and Compassion

Author: M. C. Richards

Key ideas: imagination (picturing the sufferings of others) and compassion

Rhetorical methods: analysis, cause/effect, process, argument, definition

See also: Eiseley, "The Hidden Teacher"; Eiseley, "The Sparrow Hawk"; Walker, "In Search of Our Mothers' Gardens"; Carson, "The Sense of Wonder"; Beston, "Birds"; Mueller, "What the Dog Perhaps Hears"; Holm, "The Grand Tour"; Griffin, "Use"; Merton, "Rain and the Rhinoceros"; Ozick, "The Seam of the Snail"; Didion, "On Keeping a Notebook"; Berry, "The Grandmother"; Kingston, "No Name Woman"; Silko, "Lullaby"; Ehrlich, "About Men"; Carver, "My Father's Life"; Frost, "The Death of the Hired Man"; Jeffers, "Oh, Lovely Rock"; Lopez, "The Passing Wisdom of Birds"; Momaday, "The Way to Rainy Mountain"; Jewett, "A White Heron"; Williams, "The Clan of One-Breasted Women"; Griffin, "I Like to Think of Harriet Tubman"; Morowitz, "Women's Lib and the Battle Against Entropy"; Berry, "Home of the Free"; Deloria, "We Talk, You Listen"

Comments:

90. What Is the Role of the Artist/Prophet?

Author: Walter Bruggemann

Key ideas: the artist and totalitarianism; the prophet and the king

Rhetorical methods: definition, process, cause/effect

See also: Hoff, "The Crooked Tree"; Shelley, "Ozymandias"; Abbey, "Industrial Tourism"; Thomas, "Humanities and Science"; Holm, "The Grand Tour"; Berry, "Agricultural Solutions for Agricultural Problems"; Griffin, "Use"; Merton, "Rain and the Rhinoceros"; Walker, "In Search of Our Mothers' Gardens"; Lopez, "The Passing Wisdom of Birds"; Williams, "The Clan of One-Breasted Women"; Griffin, "I Like to Think of Harriet Tubman"

Comments:

91. Matricide

Author: Matthew Fox

Key ideas: killing Mother Earth; ethical, spiritual, human issues

Rhetorical methods: argument, definition, classification

See also: Gordon and Suzuki, "How Did We Come to This?"; Gore, "Ships in the Desert"; Williams, "The Clan of One-Breasted Women"; Kerwin, "The Anatomy of Ignorance"; Thomas, "Humanities and Science"; Ferris, "The Persistence of Mystery"; Carson, "The Sense of Wonder"; Holm, "The Grand Tour"; Berry, "Agricultural Solutions for Agricultural Problems"; Griffin, "Use"; Abbey, "Industrial Tourism"; Schumacher, "Buddhist Economics"

Comments:

92. Killing Time

Author: Erich Fromm

Key idea: saving time and then killing it

Rhetorical methods: argument, definition, comparison/contrast, classification

See also: Didion, "On Keeping a Notebook"; Abbey, "The Canyon"; Merton, "Rain and the Rhinoceros"; Carson, "The Sense of Wonder"; Beston, "Birds"; Berry, "Agricultural Solutions for Agricultural Problems"; Griffin, "Use"; Ozick, "The Seam of the Snail"; Leopold, "The Deer Swath"; Jeffers, "Oh, Lovely Rock"; Jewett, "A White Heron"; Thomas, "Scabies, Scrapie"; Morowitz, "Women's Lib and the Battle Against Entropy"; Berry, "Home of the Free"; Abbey, "Industrial Tourism"; Schumacher, "Buddhist Economics"

Comments:

93. Fear

Author: Loren Eiseley

Key idea: fear

Rhetorical methods: argument, cause/effect, example

See also: Raymo, "The Silence"; Frost, "Fire and Ice"; Gordon and Suzuki, "How Did We Come to This?"; Kerwin, "The Anatomy of Ignorance"; Ferris, "The Persistence of Mystery"; Eiseley, "The Hidden Teacher"; Griffin, "Use"; Frost, "Fire and Ice"; Merton,

"Rain and the Rhinoceros"; Gordon and Suzuki, "How Did We Come to This?"; Gore, "Ships in the Desert"; Williams, "The Clan of One-Breasted Women"; Griffin, "I Like to Think of Harriet Tubman"; Abbey, "Industrial Tourism"

Comments:

94.   Who Is Fully Human?

Author: Erich Fromm

Key ideas: fully human; degeneration and suffering; growth of brain; potential

Rhetorical methods: definition, description, example, process, cause/effect, comparison/contrast, analysis

See also: Thomas, "Scabies, Scrapie"; Deloria, "We Talk, You Listen"; Carver, "My Father's Life"; Kerwin, "The Anatomy of Ignorance"; Thomas, "Humanities and Science"; Carson, "The Sense of Wonder"; Berry, "Agricultural Solutions for Agricultural Problems"; Griffin, "Use"; Lopez, "Icebergs and Cathedrals"; Merton, "Rain and the Rhinoceros"; Walker, "In Search of Our Mothers' Gardens"; Dillard, "Seeing"; Shelley, "Ozymandias"; Berry, "Home of the Free"; Abbey, "Industrial Tourism"; Schumacher, "Buddhist Economics"; Ballata, "the Mental Eye"

Comments:

95.   On Walking

Authors: Thich Nhat Hanh; Navajo prayer; Henry David Thoreau

Key ideas: walking meditation; walking in beauty; ruts in the paths of the mind

Rhetorical methods: description, narration, process, cause/effect, comparison/contrast

See also: Dillard, "Seeing"; Thoreau, "The Forest"; Carson, "The Sense of Wonder"; Eiseley, "The Hidden Teacher"; Mowat, "Naked to the Wolves"; Abbey, "The Canyon"; Merton, "Rain and the Rhinoceros"; Silko, "Lullaby"; Leopold, "The Deer Swath"; Momaday, "The Way to Rainy Mountain"; Jewett, "A White Heron"; Leopold, "Good Oak"; Williams, "The Clan of One-Breasted Women"; Abbey, "Industrial Tourism"

Comments:

96. The Power of Habit

Author: Liu I-ming

Key idea: "Contact with Rouge, Contact with Soot" parable

Rhetorical methods: process, cause/effect, argument, description, narration, example

See also: Hoff, "The Crooked Tree"; Thomas, "Humanities and Science"; Ferris, "The Persistence of Mystery"; Carson, "The Sense of Wonder"; Gregory, "Shame"; Merton, "Rain and the Rhinoceros"; Ozick, "The Seam of the Snail"; Lopez, "The Passing Wisdom of Birds"; Thomas, "Scabies, Scrapie"; Berry, "Home of the Free"; Abbey, "Industrial Tourism"; Deloria, "We Talk, You Listen"

Comments:

97. Examining "Thought Prints"

Author: Henry David Thoreau; Loren Eiseley

Key ideas: mindprints, fossil thoughts; seeing versus understanding

Rhetorical methods: description, example, analysis, cause/effect

See also: Holm, "The Grand Tour"; Lopez, "Icebergs and Cathedrals"; Lopez, "The Passing Wisdom of Birds"; Griffin, "Use"; Didion, "On Keeping a Notebook"; Walker, "In Search of Our Mothers' Gardens"; Shelley, "Ozymandias"; Momaday, "The Way to Rainy Mountain"; Leopold, "Good Oak"; Gordon and Suzuki, "How Did We Come to This?"; Gore, "Ships in the Desert"; Williams, "The Clan of One-Breasted Women"; Berry, "Home of the Free"; Abbey "Industrial Tourism"

Comments:

98. What Do Your Choices Do?

Author: Arne Naess

Key ideas: actions and thoughts are politically relevant; choices make a difference

Rhetorical methods: example, cause/effect, description

See also: Carson, "The Sense of Wonder"; Holm, "The Grand Tour"; Berry, "Agricultural Solutions for Agricultural Problems"; Griffin, "Use"; Hughes, "Theme for English B"; Gregory, "Shame"; Malcolm X, "How I Discovered Words"; Mowat, "Naked to the Wolves"; Abbey, "The Canyon"; Merton, "Rain and the

Rhinoceros"; Berry, "The Grandmother"; Walker, "In Search of Our Mothers' Gardens"; Kingston, "No Name Woman"; Silko, "Lullaby"; Ehrlich, "About Men"; Carver, "My Father's Life"; Frost, "The Death of the Hired Man"; Thoreau, "The Forest"; Dillard, "Seeing"; Leopold, "The Deer Swath"; Twain, "Two Ways of Seeing the River"; Jewett, "A White Heron"; Leopold, "Good Oak"; Gordon and Suzuki, "How Did We Come to This?"; Gore, "Ships in the Desert"; Williams, "The Clan of One-Breasted Women"; Griffin, "I Like to Think of Harriet Tubman"; Berry, "Home of the Free"; Abbey, "Industrial Tourism"; Schumacher, "Buddhist Economics"; Ballata, "The Mental Eye"

Comments:

99.   Tell and Show: A Grab Bag

Key ideas: paragraph construction; topics or thesis statements:

    Ovid—law

    Blaise Pascal—understanding and existence

    Joseph Wood Krutch—oneself for company

    Native American proverb—row away from rocks

    Kahlil Gibran—coal and diamond

    Robinson Jeffers—corruption

    Richard Nelson—one mountain a hundred times

    Aldo Leopold—right and wrong

    Omar Bradley—steer by stars

    Hector St. John de Crevecoeur—what we take up ourselves

    Pablo Casals—take part in life

    Alfred North Whitehead—simplicity on the far side of complexity

    Native American saying—living your life

    Ralph Waldo Emerson—foolish consistency

    Soren Kierkegaard—living and understanding life

    Casey Stengel—grow up but not old

    Pogo—the enemy is us

    Wendell Berry—humility and reverence

    E. F. Schumacher—destroyed by conviction of uselessness

    Edward Abbey—growth as cancer

Joseph Wood Krutch—developer as vandal of nature
E. F. Schumacher—wisdom and ignorance

100. What Can a Fact Mean?
Key idea: response writing
Jeremy Rifkin—breathing, replacement of atoms
James Lovelock—oxygen and fire
Lynn Margulis and Dorian Sagan—earth and universe; life on earth
George Eliot—hearing, vision of the ordinary
Richard Nelson—we are what we eat
Donald Culcross Peattie—man's connections to other life
John Wesley Powell—exploring the Colorado River
Richard Jefferies; D. H. Lawrence—sun always shines
Michael Furtman—water, pollution
Stephen Hawking—seeing the past in the stars
Loren Eiseley—final holocaust

Reading Reference Charts

*Author, Title, Date

*Subject/Key Idea

*Rhetorical Method(s) used in text and/or in writing exercises

*Difficulty level for college—easy, average, hard, advanced

*Page Numbers

*Dates of use and Comments or Notes from teacher

I.   Ann Kerwin—"The Anatomy of Ignorance" (1995)
Subject: the need for and value of embracing ignorance
Method: nonfiction
Difficulty: hard
Pages 131–144
Date/Comments:

I. **Lewis Thomas—"Humanities and Science" (1983)**
Subject: science, ignorance, education
Method: nonfiction—example, description, process
Difficulty: average
Pages 145–148
Date/Comments:

I. **Stephen Gould—"Darwin's Middle Road" (1980)**
Subject: science, inductivism vs. eurekaism, creativity
Method: nonfiction—description, example, contrast, process
Difficulty: average-hard
Pages 149–151
Date/Comments:

I. **Timothy Ferris—"The Persistence of Mystery" (1988)**
Subject: science, history, astronomy
Method: nonfiction—description, example, definition, process
Difficulty: advanced
Pages 152–158
Date/Comments:

I. **Rachel Carson—"The Sense of Wonder"**
Subject: education of children, value of feeling and curiosity
Method: nonfiction—example, description, process, cause/effect
Difficulty: easy
Pages 159–161
Date/Comments:

I.   **Henry Beston—"Birds" (1928)**
Subject: birds, natural order
Method: nonfiction—description, example, process
Difficulty: average-easy
Pages 162–163
Date/Comments:

I.   **Chet Raymo—"The Silence" (1985)**
Subject: astronomy, space, silence
Method: nonfiction—description, example, comparison, process
Difficulty: average-hard
Pages 164–165
Date/Comments:

I.   **Lisel Mueller—"What the Dog Perhaps Hears" (1976)**
Subject: limitations of human sense of hearing
Method: fiction—poem, comparison/contrast
Difficulty: average
Page 166
Date/Comments:

II.   **Loren Eiseley—"The Hidden Teacher" (1964)**
Subject: limitations of knowledge—spider, blood cells, human
Method: nonfiction—narration, description, example, comparison
Difficulty: average-easy, unusual point
Pages 167–169
Date/Comments:

II.   Benjamin Hoff—"The Crooked Tree" (1982)
Subject: right use, Taoism, ethics
Method: fiction—parable, narration
Difficulty: easy reading, unfamiliar idea
Page 170
Date/Comments:

II. Bill Holm—"The Grand Tour" (1985)
Subject: rural America, night, attitude toward nature, modern culture
Method: nonfiction—narration, description, example, contrast
Difficulty: average
Pages 171–172
Date/Comments:

II.   Wendell Berry—"Agricultural Solutions for Agricultural Problems" (1978)
Subject: connection between metaphor (thinking) and practical action, philosophy, technology
Method: nonfiction—description, example, cause/effect
Difficulty: average reading, complex point
Pages 173–174
Date/Comments:

II.   Susan Griffin—"Use" (1978)
Subject: science, philosophy, men's historical attitudes toward women and nature, use of chemical technology, patriarchy
Method: fiction—parable, narration, example, description, process
Difficulty: easy sentence construction, difficult concept and scientific/chemical vocabulary (essential to the point)
Pages 175–176
Date/Comments:

II. Barry Lopez—"Icebergs and Cathedrals" (1986)
Subject: history (11th, 12th, and 13th centuries), architecture, philosophy, the Arctic
Method: nonfiction—narration, example, description, definition
Difficulty: average-hard
Pages 177–179
Date/Comments:

II. Robert Frost—"Fire and Ice"
Subject: the end of the world, causes of destruction
Method: fiction—poem
Difficulty: average-easy
Page 180
Date/Comments:

III. Langston Hughes—"Theme for English B"
Subject: education, race
Method: fiction—poem, comparison/contrast
Difficulty: average-easy
Page 181
Date/Comments:

III. Dick Gregory—"Shame" (1965)
Subject: poverty, education
Method: nonfiction—narration, description, example, cause/effect, contrast
Difficulty: average-easy
Pages 183–186
Date/Comments:

III.   Malcolm X—"How I Discovered Words: A Homemade Education" (1964)

Subject: literacy, prison
Method: nonfiction—narration
Difficulty: easy
Pages 187–190
Date/Comments:

III.   Farley Mowat—"Naked to the Wolves" (1963)

Subject: wolves, Arctic, Eskimos, education
Method: nonfiction—narration, description, example, cause/effect, process
Difficulty: easy
Pages 191–195
Date/Comments:

III.   Edward Abbey—"The Canyon" (1968)

Subject: danger, desert Southwest
Method: nonfiction—narration, description, example, process, cause/effect
Difficulty: average
Pages 196–200
Date/Comments:

III.   Thomas Merton—"Rain and the Rhinoceros" (1964)

Subject: totalitarianism, solitude, Ionesco's *Rhinoceros*, mass culture
Method: nonfiction—narration, description, example, contrast, cause/effect
Difficulty: advanced
Pages 201–208
Date/Comments:

III.   Cynthia Ozick—"The Seam of the Snail"
Subject: extroverts vs. introverts, perfectionism, writing
Method: nonfiction—narrative, description, example, contrast
Difficulty: average
Pages 209–211
Date/Comments:

III.   Joan Didion—"On Keeping a Notebook"
Subject: personal reflection, "getting to know one's self"
Method: nonfiction—narrative, description, example, process, argument
Difficulty: average-hard
Pages 212–218
Date/Comments:

IV.   Wendell Berry—"The Grandmother" (1970)
Subject: rural culture (Kentucky), love
Method: fiction—poem, cause/effect
Difficulty: average
Pages 219–220
Date/Comments:

IV.   Alice Walker—"In Search of Our Mothers' Gardens" (1974)
Subject: African-American culture and history, education, creativity
Method: nonfiction—narration, description, example, cause/effect, contrast, process
Difficulty: hard-advanced
Pages 221–229
Date/Comments:

IV.   Maxine Hong Kingston—"No Name Woman" (1975)
Subject: Chinese rural culture, emigration and immigration
Method: fiction—short story
Difficulty: hard
Pages 230–239
Date/Comments:

IV.   Leslie Marmon Silko—"Lullaby" (1981)
Subject: Native American identity (Navajo), literacy and language, law, politics, poverty
Method: fiction—short story
Difficulty: average-hard
Pages 240–247
Date/Comments:

IV.   Gretel Ehrlich—"About Men" (1985)
Subject: cowboys, stereotypes, image, ranching
Method: nonfiction—narration, description, example, contrast
Difficulty: average-easy
Pages 248–250
Date/Comments:

IV.   Raymond Carver—"My Father's Life"
Subject: family life and growing up during the 1930s–1950s
Method: nonfiction—biography, narrative, process
Difficulty: average
Pages 251–257
Date/Comments:

IV.   Robert Frost—"The Death of the Hired Man" (1914)
Subject: rural culture, human relationships, home, death
Method: fiction—poem, narration
Difficulty: average
Pages 258–262
Date/Comments:

V.   Emily Dickinson—"To Make a Prairie"
Subject: power of nature and imagination
Method: fiction—poem
Difficulty: average-easy
Pages 263
Date/Comments:

V.   Bill Holm—"Horizontal Grandeur" (1985)
Subject: prairie, seeing—the prairie eye vs. the woods eye, immigration,
Method: nonfiction—narration, example, description, contrast
Difficulty: average reading level, unusual point
Pages 264–267
Date/Comments:

V.   Henry David Thoreau—"The Forest" (1858)
Subject: anticipation, preparation, and mindfulness
Method: nonfiction—narration, example, description, comparison
Difficulty: average (19th-century prose style)
Pages 268–269
Date/Comments:

V. **Annie Dillard—"Seeing" (1974)**
Subject: complexities of mindfulness and awareness
Method: nonfiction—description, example, narration, process
Difficulty: average-hard
Pages 270–276
Date/Comments:

V. **Aldo Leopold—"The Deer Swath" (1949)**
Subject: influence of habits, experience, and education on seeing
Method: nonfiction—example, description, classification, contrast
Difficulty: easy
Pages 277–278
Date/Comments:

V. **Rebecca Rupp—"Knowing the Names" (1994)**
Subject: education, seeing and vision, "amateur" science
Method: nonfiction—cause/effect, description, example, contrast
Difficulty: average-easy
Pages 279–281
Date/Comments:

V. **Samuel Clemens (Mark Twain)—"Two Ways of Seeing the River" (1883)**
Subject: Mississippi riverboat pilot, education, seeing
Method: nonfiction—contrast, description, example, cause/effect
Difficulty: average-hard (19th-century prose style, long sentences)
Pages 282–283
Date/Comments:

V.   Loren Eiseley—"The Sparrow Hawk" (1955)
Subject: birds, attitude toward nature, interpretation
Method: nonfiction—narration, description, example, process
Difficulty: average
Page 284–285
Date/Comments:

V.   Robinson Jeffers—"Oh, Lovely Rock" (1937)
Subject: seeing
Method: fiction—poem, process
Difficulty: average
Pages 286–287
Date/Comments:

VI.   Percy Bysshe Shelley—"Ozymandias"
Subject: the death of the tyrant, historical perspective
Method: fiction-poem, narrative
Difficulty: average
Page 288
Date/Comment:

VI.   Barry Lopez—"The Passing Wisdom of Birds" (1985)
Subject: history of conquest of the Aztecs (1519–1521), Western value systems, philosophy
Method: nonfiction—narration, description, example, process, cause/effect
Difficulty: average-hard
Pages 289–293
Date/Comments:

VI. **N. Scott Momaday—Prologue and Introduction to *The Way to Rainy Mountain* (1969)**
Subject: Kiowa history; memory, experience, and myth
Method: nonfiction—narration, description, example, process
Difficulty: average-easy
Pages 294–300
Date/Comments:

VI. **Sarah Orne Jewett—"A White Heron" (1886)**
Subject: 19th-century natural science; attitudes toward nature; uneducated, rural vs. educated, urban culture
Method: fiction—short story
Difficulty: easy
Pages 301–308
Date/Comments:

VI. **Aldo Leopold—"Good Oak" (1949)**
Subject: American history and culture
Method: nonfiction—narration, description, example, process, cause/effect
Difficulty: average
Pages 309–315
Date/Comments:

VI. **Anita Gordon and David Suzuki—"How Did We Come To This?" (1990)**
Subject: human history, philosophy, environmental degradation, science
Method: nonfiction—description, example, process, cause/effect
Difficulty: average
Pages 316–323
Date/Comments:

VI.   Al Gore—"Ships in the Desert" (1992)

Subject: worldwide, man-made environmental changes; politics; population

Method: nonfiction—narration, description, example, process, cause/effect

Difficulty: average

Pages 324–327

Date/Comments:

VI.   Terry Tempest Williams—"The Clan of One-Breasted Women" (1990)

Subject: nuclear testing, cancer, politics, religion

Method: nonfiction—narration, description, example, cause/effect, process

Difficulty: average—emotionally powerful

Pages 328–334

Date/Comments:

VII.   Susan Griffin—"I Like to Think of Harriet Tubman" (1976)

Subject: Harriet Tubman, slavery, poverty, attitudes toward women, law

Method: fiction—poem

Difficulty: average

Pages 335–337

Date/Comments:

VII.   Lewis Thomas—"Scabies, Scrapie" (1983)

Subject: marriage, leadership, education

Method: nonfiction—narration, description, example, process

Difficulty: average

Pages 338–341

Date/Comments:

Part Two: Reference Charts

VI. Harold Morowitz—"Women's Lib and the Battle Against Entropy" (1979)
Subject: science, culture, equality
Method: nonfiction—narration, description, example, process, cause/effect, definition
Difficulty: average-hard
Pages 342–344
Date/Comments:

VII. Wendell Berry—"Home of the Free" (1978)
Subject: technology, American culture, elitism
Method: nonfiction—description, example, cause/effect, process
Difficulty: average-hard
Pages 345–349
Date/Comments:

VII. Edward Abbey—"Industrial Tourism" (1968)
Subject: national parks, history, attitude toward nature, technology, law
Method: nonfiction—description, example, cause/effect, contrast, process, definition
Difficulty: average-hard
Pages 350–358
Date/Comments:

VII. Vine Deloria, Jr.—"We Talk, You Listen" (1970)
Subject: Native American identity, history, mass media, education
Method: nonfiction—description, example, cause/effect, process
Difficulty: average
Pages 359–366
Date/Comments:

VII.   E. F. Schumacher—"Buddhist Economics" (1966)
Subject: economics, right use, limitations, intermediate technology
Method: nonfiction—description, example, contrast
Difficulty: average-hard
Pages 367–374
Date/Comments:

Phyllis Ballata—"The Mental Eye" (1995)
Subject: education, the necessity and value of the thought process, meaning vs. know-how
Method: nonfiction—example, cause/effect, process, persuasion
Difficulty: advanced
Pages 408–412
Date/Comments:

Rhetorical Methods Used in the Writing Projects (Part One)
(desc=description; ex=example; narr=narration; class=classification/division; c/c=compare/contrast; pro=process; c/e=cause/effect; def=definition; arg=argument; ana=analysis)

	desc	ex	narr	class	c/c	pro	c/e	def	arg	ana
1. Collecting and Connecting		b	b		a			d	c	
2. What is Education		c				c	c	a, b		
3. On Grief		a, b, c	a, b, c			c	a, b, c			c
4. "What You See Is..."		b			a	b		c		
5. The Meaning of Rich					b, c			a, b, c		b
6. On Journeys		a			b, c	c, d	c, d	c	b, c	d
7. On Leadership					a, b	b	b	c		
8. Foreseeing and Forestalling		b, c				b, c	b, c	a		
9. On Judging Quality		a	a, b			a, b				
10. Are We "Tools of Our Tools"?		b	b			a	a, b, d	c		c
11. On Specialization		c		e			a, d	d	b, c	a
12. "See No Evil": Facing Facts		•	•			•	•			
13. What Do We Owe...					b		a	a	b	
14. The Value of Mistakes			c				c	a	b, d	
15. On the "Mental Eye"								a, b		a

92   Part Two: Reference Charts

	desc	ex	narr	class	c/c	pro	c/e	def	arg	ana
16. Engaging Contraries					b		c	a		a
17. Making Things Come Alive			a				a, b	b		b
18. Standing Up For—What?		b	b			a		a	b	
19. Truth?		c, e	d		a, c, e			c, b, e	c	a, c
20. On Respect				c		a, b	a, b, c	a, b, c	c	
21. On Seeing	•									•
22. Can the Worthwhile Be...			b	a	b, c	b	a			
23. What is Required...			a			a, b	a, b			b
24. On Affluence				b	b, c			a, b, c		
25. On Literacy	a	a	b, e	h	d, f	b, e	c, f, g	h	f	
26. What Is Too Much					•		•		•	
27. Planting Barley, Harvesting...		•	•				•			
28. On Order			•			•	•			
29. The Value of Limits			b		a	c	c	b	c	
30. On Day and Night	a, b		a		b					
31. Color	•				•					
32. Friendhip		•					•	•		

Part Two: Reference Charts 93

	desc	ex	narr	class	c/c	pro	c/e	def	arg	ana
33. Preventing Problems...			•			•				
34. On Caring		a	a		b	c	c			
35. On Awareness			•			•	•			
36. Seeing "Near and Narrowly"	•				•					
37. Looking versus Seeing	•									
38. What Is a Good Education?								•		
39. The Experience of Art...					•					
40. The Importance of Ignorance		•		•						•
41. On Thinking			•				•			
42. On Learning to Love Life		a			b, c	a	d, e, f			
43. Time			•			•				
44. Conquering	•						•			
45. Excellence					c, e	a	a, b, d	a, d		
46. Aiming		a	b		a		b		b	a
47. The Centrifugal and...					b	a, b				
48. What Does Television Provide?									•	
49. What is "Right"?					b			a, b	b	b

94   Part Two: Reference Charts

	desc	ex	narr	class	c/c	pro	c/e	def	arg	ana
50. Irony	b							b	a	
51. Fact versus Interpretation					a, c				b, d	a, c
52. Seeing What Is There...	a	f				c, f	a, d, e	b		
53. What's in a Word?				b			a, d	a, b, c		d
54. Making What's Difficult...			a		b	a, b	b			
55. On Reading	a				b					
56. On Finding the Essence	•					•				
57. The Aims of Advertising	a, b			a, b	c		a			
58. On Doing Work You Love						•	•			
59. Preparing for Good Luck						•	•			
60. Asking the Right Questions						•	•			
61. Being Alone	c	a, c		c	b		a, b	b		a
62. Knowing One's Self					a, b			b		a
63. Defining Freedom								•		
64. One for All or One for One		b		a	b	a				
65. Do Unto Others					b, c		a, c		c	
66. What Is Happiness?	b				b, d		b	a, b, e	c	

Part Two: Reference Charts   95

	desc	ex	narr	class	c/c	pro	c/e	def	arg	ana
67. Means and Ends					c	b, c		a	b	a
68. Words and Ideas	b	b			c		a, b		b, c	
69. Enjoyments					a	a, b	a, b		b	
70. What Should Work Be?	c						a, b	a, b, c		b
71. On Recreation	•		•							•
72. What Are Stories For?					c, f			a, b, d, e		
73. Are You Raw of Cooked?	a				a, b					
74. On Taking Your Time			c, d		b	c, d	c, d		a	
75. "The Proper University..."					a			b		
76. On Spiritual Fruit					b			a, b		
77. Whose Shoulders Are You...	•		•							
78. On Growing Old		b	b, d	e	d	a, b, d, e	c	a		
79. Sin and Virtue							a, b	a, b, c		
80. Is "Know-How" Enough?	a	b, d	d	b	c	a, b, c, d	c	a		
81. On Leveling Down	b						b	a, c	b	
82. Keeping Your Thought		a, b	a			b	b			
83. A Question of Conscience...						a, b, c	a, b, c, d		b, c, d	

Part Two: Reference Charts

	desc	ex	narr	class	c/c	pro	c/e	def	arg	ana
84. On Appearance and Reality							a, b, c, d, e		a, b, c, d, e, f	
85. Wasting the Body, Wasting...									a, b, c, d, e	
86. On Appetite and Anticipation						d	a, b, d	c	c	
87. Are You Fenced In?						a	a, c, d		b	a
88. And Who Is My Neighbor	a	a				b		a	b, c	
89. On Imagination...						a	a	c, d	b	a
90. What Is the Role...?						d, e, f	d, e, f	a, b, c, d, e, f		
91. Matricide			e					b, c, d	a	
92. Killing Time			e	d				c	a, b	
93. Fear		c					b, c		a	
94. Who is Fully Human?	b	b			d	c, d	c	a		b
95. On Walking	•		•		•	•	•			
96. The Power of Habit	b	b	b			a	a		a	
97. Examining "Thought Prints"	•	•					•			•
98. What Do Your Choices Do?	•	•					•			•

Part Two: Reference Charts   97

	desc	ex	narr	class	c/c	pro	c/e	def	arg	ana
99. Tell and Show...					4, 7, 8, 9, 11, 15, 16, 21	3, 4, 7, 8, 9, 10, 13, 15, 16, 18, 22	1, 2, 8, 9, 10, 13, 14, 16, 17, 19, 20, 22	5, 12, 14, 17, 18, 19, 21, 22	1, 6, 7, 10, 11, 12, 17, 18, 19, 20, 21, 22	
100. What Can a Fact Mean?	•	•	•				•	•		•

Rhetorical Methods Used in the Writing Projects (Part Two)

	desc	ex	narr	class	c/c	pro	c/e	def	arg	ana
Seeing Ignorance										
The Anatomy of Ignorance (Kerwin 131–144)		•		•	•	•		•	•	
Humanities and Science (Thomas 145–148)						•			•	
Darwin's Middle Road (Gould (149–151)					•	•		•	•	
The Persistence of Mystery (Ferris 152–158)		•				•		•	•	
The Sense of Wonder (Carson 159–161)						•	•		•	
Birds (Beston 162–163)	•	•	•			•		•		
The Silence (Raymo 164–165)	•	•					•			
What the Dog Perhaps Hears (Mueller 166)		•					•			

Part Two: Reference Charts

	desc	ex	narr	class	c/c	pro	c/e	def	arg	ana
Seeing Metaphors										
The Hidden Teacher (Eiseley 167–169)	•	•	•		•		•			
The Crooked Tree (Hoff 170)		•	•		•			•		
The Grand Tour (Holm 171–172)	•	•	•		•					
Agricultural Solutions (Berry 173–174)					•		•			
Use (Griffin 175–176)		•			•	•	•			
Icebergs and Cathedrals (Lopez 177–179)	•	•			•	•				
Fire and Ice (Frost 180)					•		•			
Seeing Ourselves										
Theme for English B (Hughes 181–182)	•	•			•		•			
Shame (Gregory 183–186)			•			•	•			
How I Discovered Words (Malcolm X 187–190)			•			•	•			
Naked to the Wolves (Mowat 191–195)			•		•	•	•			
The Canyon (Abbey 196–200)	•		•			•	•			
Rain and the Rhinocerous (Merton 201–208)	•	•	•	•		•			•	
The Seam of the Snail (Ozick 209–211)		•			•			•		

Part Two: Reference Charts   99

	desc	ex	narr	class	c/c	pro	c/e	def	arg	ana
On Keeping a Notebook (Didion 212–218)	•	•				•				
Seeing Others										
The Grandmother (Berry 219–220)	•				•		•			
In Search of Our Mothers' Gardens (Walker (221–229)			•			•	•			
No Name Woman (Kingston 230–239)	•		•				•			
Lullaby (Silko 240–247)	•		•			•	•			
About Men (Erlich 248–250)	•							•		
My Father's Life (Carver 251–257)			•			•				
The Death of the Hired Man (Frost 258–262)			•			•		•		
Seeing Nature										
To Make a Prarie (Dickinson 263)								•		
Horizontal Grandeur (Holm 264–267)	•				•				•	
The Forest (Thoreau 268–269)	•	•			•				•	
Seeing (Dillard 270–276)	•	•	•			•	•		•	
The Deer Swath (Leopold 277–278)				•						
Knowing the Names (Rupp 279–281)		•				•	•	•		

	desc	ex	narr	class	c/c	pro	c/e	def	arg	ana
Two Ways of Seeing the River (Twain 282–283)	•	•			•					
The Sparrow Hawk (Eiseley 284–285)	•		•			•				
Oh, Lovely Rock (Jeffers 286–287)	•		•							
Seeing the Past										
Ozymandias (Shelley 288)		•				•		•		
The Passing Wisdom of Birds (Lopez 289–293)	•		•			•				
The Way to Rainy Mountain (Momaday 294–300)	•		•			•				
A White Heron (Jewett 301–308)	•		•		•	•	•			
Good Oak (Leopold 309–315)		•		•		•				
How Did We Come to This? (Gordon and Suzuki 316–323)		•			•	•	•		•	
Ships in the Desert (Gore 324–327)		•	•				•			
The Clan of the One-Breasted Women (Williams 328–334)		•	•				•		•	
From Seeing to Persuading										
I Like to Think of Harriet Tubman (Griffin 335–337)		•			•		•		•	
Scabies, Scrapie (Thomas 338–341)		•		•					•	

Part Two: Reference Charts 101

	desc	ex	narr	class	c/c	pro	c/e	def	arg	ana
Women's Lib and... (Morowitz 342–344)			•			•	•	•	•	
Home of the Free (Berry 345–349)		•					•	•	•	
Industrial Tourism (Abbey 350–358)				•	•	•	•	•	•	
We Talk, You Listen (Deloria 359–366)		•		•	•		•		•	
Buddhist Economics (Schumacher 367–374)				•	•		•		•	

Reading and Writing Projects Organized by Rhetorical Methods

Describing

Readings
Birds—Beston (162)
The Silence—Raymo (164)
The Hidden Teacher—Eiseley (167)
The Grand Tour—Holm (171)
Icebergs and Cathedrals—Lopez (177)
Theme for English B—Hughes (181)
The Canyon—Abbey (196)
Rain and the Rhinoceros—Merton (201)
On Keeping a Notebook—Joan Didion (212)
The Grandmother—Berry (219)
No Name Woman—Kingston (230)
Lullaby—Silko (240)
About Men—Erhlich (248)
Horizontal Grandeur—Holm (264)
The Forest—Thoreau (268)
Seeing—Dillard (270)
Two Ways of Seeing the River—Twain (282)
The Sparrow Hawk—Eiseley (284)
Oh, Lovely Rock—Jeffers (286)
The Passing Wisdom of Birds—Lopez (289)
The Way to Rainy Mountain—Momaday (294)
A White Heron—Jewett (301)

Writing Projects for Describing

16a	21	25a	30a	31	36	37	44	50b
52a	55a	56	57a	57b	61c	66b	68b	70c
71	73a	77	80a	81b	88a	94b	95	96b
97	98	99	100					

Using Examples

Readings
The Anatomy of Ignorance—Kerwin (131)
The Persistence of Mystery—Ferris (152)
Birds—Beston (162)
The Silence—Raymo (164)
What the Dog Perhaps Hears—Mueller (166)
The Hidden Teacher—Eiseley (167)
The Crooked Tree—Hoff (170)
The Grand Tour—Holm (171)

Part Two: Reference Charts 103

Icebergs and Cathedrals—Lopez (177)
Theme for English B—Hughes (181)
Rain and the Rhinoceros—Merton (201)
The Seam of the Snail—Ozick (209)
On Keeping a Notebook—Didion (212)
No Name Woman—Kingston (230)
About Men—Ehrlich (248)
The Forest—Thoreau (268)
Seeing—Dillard (270)
Knowing the Names—Rupp (279)
Two Ways of Seeing the River—Twain (282)
Good Oak—Leopold (309)
How Did We Come to This?—Gordon and Suzuki (316)
Ships in the Desert—Gore (324)
The Clan of One-Breasted Women—Williams (328)
I Like to Think of Harriet Tubman—Griffin (335)
Scabies, Scrapie—Thomas (338)
Home of the Free—Berry (345)
We Talk, You Listen—Deloria (359)

Writing Projects for Using Examples

1b	2c	3a	3b	3c	4c	6a	8b	8c	9a
10b	11c	12	18b	19c	19e	25a	27	32	34a
40	42a	46a	52f	61a	61c	65b	68b	78b	80a
80d	82a	82b	88a	93c	94b	96b	97	98	99
100									

Narrating

Readings
Birds—Beston (162)
The Hidden Teacher—Eiseley (167)
The Crooked Tree—Hoff (170)
The Grand Tour—Holm (171)
Use—Griffin (175)
Shame—Gregory (183)
How I Discovered Words—Malcolm X (187)
Naked to the Wolves—Mowat (191)
The Canyon—Abbey (196)
Rain and the Rhinoceros—Merton (201)
In Search of Our Mothers' Gardens—Walker (221)
No Name Woman—Kingston (230)
Lullaby—Silko (240)
My Father's Life—Carver (251)
The Death of the Hired Man—Frost (258)
Seeing—Dillard (270)
The Sparrow Hawk—Eiseley (284)
Oh, Lovely Rock—Jeffers (286)

Ozymandias—Shelley (288)
The Passing Wisdom of Birds—Lopez (289)
The Way to Rainy Mountain—Momaday (294)
A White Heron—Jewett (301)
Ships in the Desert—Gore (324)
The Clan of One-Breasted Women—Williams (328)
Women's Lib and the Battle Against Entropy—Morowitz (342)

Writing Projects for Narrating

1b	3a	3b	3c	9a	9b	10b	12	14c	17a
18b	19d	22b	23a	25b	25e	27	28	29b	30a
30b	33	34a	35	41	43	46b	54a	71	74c
74d	77	78b	78d	80d	82a	95	96b	100	

Classifying and Dividing

Readings
The Anatomy of Ignorance—Kerwin (131)
Rain and the Rhinoceros—Merton (201)
The Deer Swath—Leopold (277)
Good Oak—Leopold (309)
Industrial Tourism—Abbey (350)
We Talk, You Listen—Deloria (359)
Buddhist Economics—Schumacher (367)

Writing Projects for Classifying and Dividing

| 11e | 20c | 22a | 24b | 25h | 40 | 57a | 57b | 61c | 64a |
| 78e | 80b | 91e | 92e | | | | | | |

Comparing and Contrasting

Readings
The Anatomy of Ignorance—Kerwin (131)
Darwin's Middle Road—Gould (149)
The Hidden Teacher—Eiseley (167)
The Crooked Tree—Hoff (170)
The Grand Tour—Holm (171)
Agricultural Solutions for Agricultural Problems—Berry (173)
Use—Griffin (175)
Icebergs and Cathedrals—Lopez (177)
Fire and Ice—Frost (180)
Theme for English B—Hughes (181)
Naked to the Wolves—Mowat (191)
The Seam of the Snail—Ozick (209)
The Grandmother—Berry (219)
Horizontal Grandeur—Holm (264)

The Forest—Thoreau (268)
Two Ways of Seeing the River—Twain (282)
A White Heron—Jewett (301)
How Did We Come to This?—Gordon and Suzuki (316)
I Like to Think of Harriet Tubman—Griffin (335)
Scabies, Scrapie—Thomas (338)
We Talk, You Listen—Deloria (359)
Industrial Tourism—Abbey (350)
Buddhist Economics—Schumacher (367)

Writing Projects for Comparing and Contrasting

1a	4a	5b	5c	6b	6c	7a	7b	13b	16b
19a	19c	19e	22b	22c	24b	24c	25d	25f	26
29a	30b	31	34b	36	39	42b	42c	45c	45e
46a	47b	49b	51a	51c	53b	54b	55b	57c	61
64b	65b	65c	66b	66d	67c	68c	69a	72c	72f
73a	73b	74b	75b	76b	78d	80c	87a	92d	94d
95	99								

Explaining a Process

Readings

The Anatomy of Ignorance—Kerwin (131)
Humanities and Science—Thomas (145)
Darwin's Middle Road—Gould (149)
The Persistence of Mystery—Ferris (152)
The Sense of Wonder—Carson (159)
Birds—Beston (162)
Use—Griffin (175)
Icebergs and Cathedrals—Lopez (177)
Shame—Gregory (183)
How I Discovered Words—Malcolm X (187)
Naked to the Wolves—Mowat (191)
The Canyon—Abbey (196)
Rain and the Rhinoceros—Merton (201)
On Keeping a Notebook—Didion (212)
In Search of Our Mothers' Gardens—Walker (221)
Lullaby—Silko (240)
My Father's Life—Carver (251)
The Death of the Hired Man—Frost (258)
Seeing—Dillard (270)
Knowing the Names—Rupp (279)
The Sparrow Hawk—Eiseley (284)
Ozymandias—Shelley (288)
The Passing Wisdom of Birds—Lopez (289)
The Way to Rainy Mountain—Momaday (294)
A White Heron—Jewett (301)
Good Oak—Leopold (309)

106　　Part Two: Reference Charts

How Did We Come to This?—Gordon and Suzuki (316)
Women's Lib and the Battle Against Entropy—Morowitz (342)
Industrial Tourism—Abbey (350)

Writing Projects for Explaining a Process

2c	3c	4b	6c	6d	7b	8b	8c	9a	9b
10a	12	18a	20a	20b	22b	23a	23b	25b	25e
28	29c	33	34c	35	42a	43	45a	47a	47b
52c	52f	54a	54b	56	58	59	60a	60b	62a
62b	64a	67b	67c	69a	69b	74c	74d	78a	78b
78d	78e	80a	80b	80c	80d	82b	83a	83b	83c
86d	88b	89a	90d	90e	90f	94c	94d	95	96a
99	100								

Explaining Cause and Effect

Readings
The Sense of Wonder—Carson (159)
The Silence—Raymo (164)
What the Dog Perhaps Hears—Mueller (166)
The Hidden Teacher—Eiseley (167)
Agricultural Solutions to Agricultural Problems—Berry (173)
Use—Griffin (175)
Icebergs and Cathedrals—Lopez (177)
Fire and Ice—Frost (180)
Theme for English B—Hughes (181)
Shame—Gregory (183)
How I Discovered Words—Malcolm X (187)
Naked to the Wolves—Mowat (191)
The Canyon—Abbey (196)
The Grandmother—Berry (219)
In Search of Our Mothers' Gardens—Walker (221)
No Name Woman—Kingston (230)
Lullaby—Silko (240)
Seeing—Dillard (270)
Knowing the Names—Rupp (279)
A White Heron—Jewett (301)
How Did We Come to This?—Gordon and Suzuki (316)
Ships in the Desert—Al Gore (324)
The Clan of One-Breasted Women—Williams (328)
I Like to Think of Harriet Tubman—Griffin (335)
Women's Lib and the Battle Against Entropy (342)
Home of the Free—Berry (345)
Industrial Tourism—Abbey (350)
We Talk, You Listen—Deloria (359)
Buddhist Economics—Schumacher (367)

Part Two: Reference Charts   107

Writing Projects for Explaining Cause and Effect

2c	3a	3b	3c	6c	6d	7b	8b	10a	10b
10d	11a	11d	12	13a	14c	16c	17a	17b	20a
20b	20c	22a	23a	23b	25c	25f	25g	26	27
28	29c	32	34c	35	41	42d	42e	42f	44
45a	45b	45d	46b	52a	52d	52e	53a	53d	54b
57a	58	59	60b	61a	61b	65a	65c	66b	68a
68b	69a	69b	70a	70b	74c	74d	78c	79a	79b
80c	81b	82b	83a	83b	83c	83d	84a	84b	84c
84d	84e	86a	86b	86d	87a	87c	89a	90d	90e
90f	93b	93c	94c	95	96a	97	98	99	100

Defining

Readings
The Anatomy of Ignorance—Kerwin (131)
Darwin's Middle Road—Gould (149)
The Persistence of Mystery—Ferris (152)
Birds—Beston (162)
The Crooked Tree—Hoff (170)
The Seam of the Snail—Ozick (209)
About Men—Ehrlich (248)
The Death of the Hired Man—Frost (258)
To Make a Prairie—Dickinson (263)
Knowing the Names—Rupp (279)
Ozymandias—Shelley (288)
Women's Lib and the Battle Against Entropy—Morowitz (342)
Home of the Free—Berry (345)
Industrial Tourism—Abbey (350)
Buddhist Economics—Schumacher (367)

Writing Projects for Defining

2a	2b	4c	5a	5b	5c	6c	7c	8a	10c
11d	13a	14a	15a	15b	17b	18a	19b	19c	19e
20a	20b	20c	24a	24b	24c	25h	29b	32	38
45a	45d	49a	49b	50b	52b	53a	53b	53c	61b
63	66a	66b	66e	67a	70a	70b	70c	72a	72b
72d	72e	75a	76a	76b	78a	79a	79b	79c	80a
81a	82c	86c	88a	89c	89d	90a	90b	90c	90d
90e	90f	91b	91c	91d	92c	94a	99		